LEGENDS GUIDE TO THE

GOLF COURSES
OF HILTON HEAD ISLAND

LEGENDS GUIDE TO THE
GOLF COURSES
OF HILTON HEAD ISLAND

LEGENDS PUBLICATIONS
Hilton Head Island, South Carolina

Edited by Eileen Lockwood
Book and cover design by AlphaBets Design Inc.
Page illustrations by Scott Bunting and Betsy Bayley
Photography by Bill Littell
Photos on pages 113, 114, 134, & 154 contributed by Dunes Marketing.

Printed in Hong Kong by Hindy's Enterprise Co. Ltd.

ISBN 0-9627893-0-5

Library of Congress Catalog Card Number 91-090041

Ideas are simply possibilities
that should be taken advantage of.
It is great to know so many
that can help to make
the possibilities
a reality.

Table of Contents

The Legend

Every hole of every golf course currently on Hilton Head Island, has been photographed and illustrated within this book. The photographs are from various angles, providing an interesting view of the hole. The diagrams show all relevant sand bunkers, mounds and trees from tee to green.

Green measurements, in yards, are displayed in a box, either right or left of the diagram. The horizontal line (—) measures the width of the green and the vertical line (|) measures the depth. Note that these numbers indicate the longest distance from side to side and front to back. Such that a non-circular green is measured as:

Basic yardages (100, 150, 200 and etc . . .) set to the side of the diagram and point to the respective location on the hole

The legend below is a guide to the symbols of features related to the various holes.

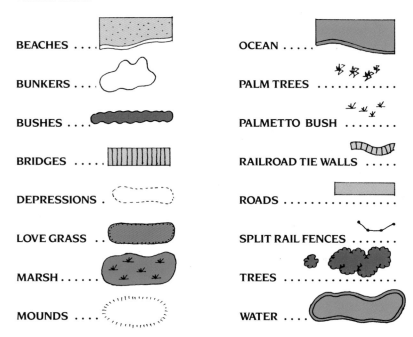

BEACHES . . . .

BUNKERS . . . .

BUSHES . . . .

BRIDGES . . . . .

DEPRESSIONS .

LOVE GRASS . .

MARSH . . . . . .

MOUNDS . . . .

OCEAN . . . . .

PALM TREES . . . .

PALMETTO BUSH . . . .

RAILROAD TIE WALLS . . . . .

ROADS . . . .

SPLIT RAIL FENCES . . . .

TREES . . . .

WATER . . . .

Introduction

Hilton Head Island is located at the southeastern corner of South Carolina. The island enjoys some of the most beautiful weather year-round. In summer months soft ocean breezes mitigate the heat. In winter, temperatures rarely get below 60 degrees. The unique coastal region blesses the island with sunny splendor and dark rain clouds are seldom seen. This tropical clime is ideal for the growth of the many pines, magnificent magnolias, numerous palm trees and the unique Spanish Moss that hangs from the tree limbs everywhere on the island. Naturally, these characteristics help to make this an excellent area for the outstanding courses that make this a literal golfer's paradise.

Exactly how many courses are on the island, and what are they like? This question was the motivation for producing this book. The idea was to assemble the most comprehensive guide to the golf courses of Hilton Head Island. Before he or she steps up to the first tee, the avid golfer can become familiar with each course, first by reading an introduction describing the characteristics that make it unique, and then by examining the photographs, diagrams and text that offer guidelines to playing each hole. Finally, a map of each course is provided to show each hole relative to the others. Status of the course, private or public, is also listed on this last page, along with the statistcal information such as hole by hole yardages, ratings, and pertinent names. Overall, this guide should provide a complete picture of each golf course on Hilton Head Island.

Using this book should prove to be fun and beneficial. Those who are unfamiliar with the various golf courses on the island will be able to glance through and get a good feel for what the island has to offer. Those who know the courses may find helpful hints on how to play each of them. The format makes it easy to take an inside look at all the courses on Hilton Head Island. The photographs show each hole in color, the diagrams reveal each hole's yardages and features, and the text gives pointers on how to play the hole. By taking a brief look at a course presented in this book, a golfer should be well prepared to take on the challenges that each golf course has to offer.

There is a total of twenty separate golf course layouts. This includes each of Shipyard Plantation's nine-hole courses, as well as Spanish Wells' nine-hole design. A total of 354 holes are open for play, as of this publication date, and three more courses are in preparation to bring the total number of golf courses on the island to twenty-three.

The Plantation

The second largest plantation on Hilton Head Island, Hilton Head Plantation is located on the northwest corner of the island. 3,918 acres provide ample room for four golf courses and many residential homes. The plantation has the unique characteristic of having the highest point on the island at 28.24 feet above sea level. The location affords various scenic views, from the golf courses, of Port Royal Sound and the U.S. Intercoastal Waterway. The many pines and the rolling geography provide a perfect setting for some interesting golf layouts. Two totally private golf courses and two semi-private courses are found within the gates. The courses are as follows:

Bear Creek Golf Club

Dolphin Head Golf Club

Hilton Head Country Club

Oyster Reef Golf Club

BEAR CREEK GOLF CLUB

The Course

This course was designed by Rees Jones in 1978 and has been modified with the help of Arthur Hills since then. Bear Creek is located just inside the gate to Hilton Head Plantation. Like the other totally private courses on the island, Bear Creek is an exceptional golf course. The layout is tough from the start, long narrow fairways demand the golfer's undivided attention. The rolling fairways play to medium sized undulating greens. A solid golf game from tee to green is a necessity on this course.

On the front nine you are immediately confronted with three tough golf holes, which means you should be in your best game form. The par 4 first hole demands accuracy on the approach. The second hole, par 3, establishes the importance of hitting the green in regulation. The third, at a long 426 yards, reveals the worthiness of the 'Bear'. The fourth, fifth, sixth and seventh settle down a bit, allowing for possible birdies. The eighth and ninth complete the nine with unsympathetic requests. The eighth green is hidden from view at the tee, requiring a blind shot to the putting surface. The ninth wraps up the front at 430 yards, usually into the wind!

After the front, most players will need an energy replenishment before venturing off to the back nine. The 'Bear' does not relax its demands on the final nine holes. Medium-length holes still require planning in order to keep the ball in the fairway and on course for the cup. Staying away from the trees will not only help keep the score down, but it will also help to avoid meeting any bears! The course finishes with a narrow par 5, requiring an approach over a large pond.

BEAR CREEK GOLF CLUB

	BLUE	WHITE	GREEN	RED
YDS:	360	326	314	310
PAR:	4	4	4	4
HDCP:	15	15	15	11

1

Although not very long, the first hole of Bear Creek reveals the characteristics of the course to come. A fairway bunker found on the left side encourages the golfer to hit the drive down the right side. However, be warned of the water that lurks to the right.

A careful shot down the middle is the key. The approach is to a small flat green which is protected by both sand and grass bunkers. Played conservatively, this first hole should be a confidence builder.

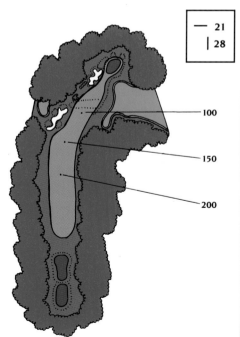

— 21
| 28

100

150

200

BEAR CREEK GOLF CLUB

2

	BLUE	WHITE	GREEN	RED
YDS:	161	134	107	102
PAR:	3	3	3	3
HDCP:	17	17	17	17

—— 20
| 34

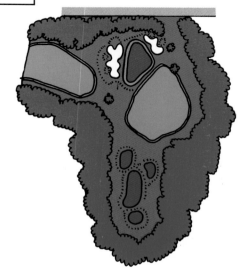

Water is the main ingredient on this par three. Play the safe shot; aim right for the center of the green. It is not necessary, or well advised, to be concerned with the water or sandtraps which lurk around the green.

As with all par threes, the wind can ruin a well hit shot. Take your time and adjust your shot to the speed and direction of the wind.

BEAR CREEK GOLF CLUB

	BLUE	WHITE	GREEN	RED
YDS:	426	394	369	338
PAR:	4	4	4	4
HDCP:	1	1	1	1

3

Fairway bunkers abound in the target area on this hole. Drives left or right of the fairway will probably find the sand.

A drive down the right side, drawing back to the middle, is the optimal shot here. Mounding and water down the left side will lead you to the right, but be careful of the sandtrap situated to the right of the green.

A larger green than the first two, this third is slightly elevated and flat. Putts will fall easily.

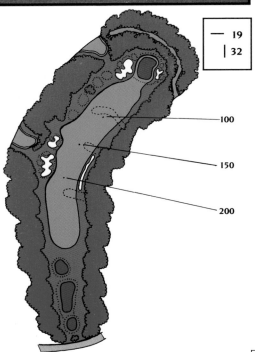

— 19
| 32

—100

—150

—200

BEAR CREEK GOLF CLUB

4

	BLUE	WHITE	GREEN	RED
YDS:	515	485	457	427
PAR:	5	5	5	5
HDCP:	5	5	5	3

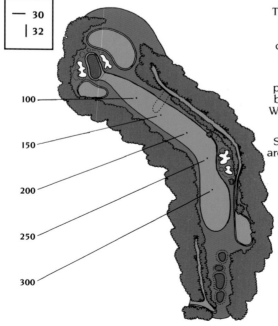

This first par five confirms Bear Creek as a worthy challenge. Fairway bunkers on the right outside corner guide drives to the more appealing left side.

Driving down the the left will prepare for the second shot to be played down the right side. Water right and left of the green is not really a threat here.

Shallow green rolls left. Birdies are not unrespectable on this hole.

	BLUE	WHITE	GREEN	RED
YDS:	341	334	303	292
PAR:	4	4	4	4
HDCP:	11	11	11	13

5

This fifth is a short par four, but difficult nonetheless. Accuracy off the tee is a must. Right center fairway is most favorable. Large grass bunkers sweep in from the left side.

The approach is made to a green which is protected by bunkers short left and right.

The green slopes forward and gives the illusion of being shorter than it actually is. Slippery downhill and sidehill putts can be expected if the ball is hit past the cup on the approach.

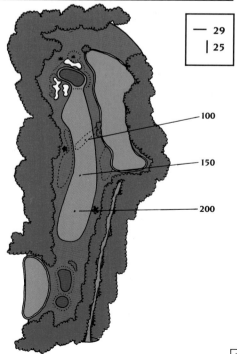

— 29
| 25

100

150

200

BEAR CREEK GOLF CLUB

6

	BLUE	WHITE	GREEN	RED
YDS:	389	357	341	322
PAR:	4	4	4	4
HDCP:	9	9	9	9

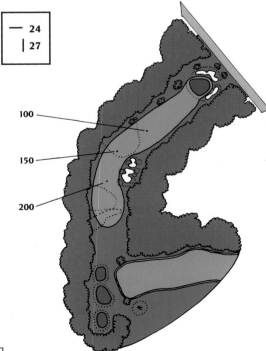

— 24
| 27

100

150

200

The sixth is a little longer than the fifth. As you can see from the picture, it is not a good idea to cut the corner — unless a large drive is hit. The probability of landing in one of these bunkers is strong.

The more traditional way to play the hole is with a drive down the left middle of the fairway. Once around the corner, the wind picks up. Plan on using a long iron to get to the green.

The green elevated but flat, a signal that all putts are makeable.

BEAR CREEK GOLF CLUB

	BLUE	WHITE	GREEN	RED
YDS:	505	478	436	410
PAR:	5	5	5	5
HDCP:	3	3	3	7

7

Another picture from the corner of the dogleg. Mounding at this corner can draw balls back into the fairway, but also ricochet them into the woods!

Play wisely by aiming the drive down the left middle of the fairway. But be careful. Bunkers at the top side of the corner will grab any drive over 210 yards.

The second shot is of no real concern. Keep the ball left, out of the marsh coming in from the right.

The approach can be tricky. The green is elevated and slightly undulated. Bunkers all around are eager to snatch misplaced shots. Par is good, but birdies are not to be ruled out.

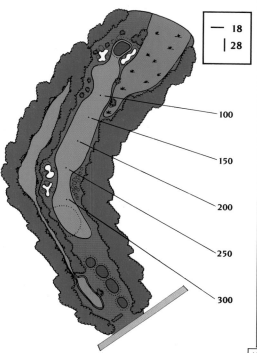

BEAR CREEK GOLF CLUB

8

	BLUE	WHITE	GREEN	RED
YDS:	189	165	124	104
PAR:	3	3	3	3
HDCP:	13	13	13	15

— 26
| 29

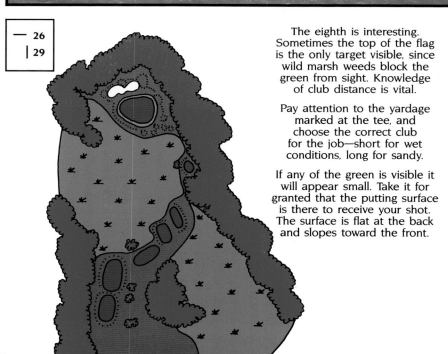

The eighth is interesting. Sometimes the top of the flag is the only target visible, since wild marsh weeds block the green from sight. Knowledge of club distance is vital.

Pay attention to the yardage marked at the tee, and choose the correct club for the job—short for wet conditions, long for sandy.

If any of the green is visible it will appear small. Take it for granted that the putting surface is there to receive your shot. The surface is flat at the back and slopes toward the front.

BEAR CREEK GOLF CLUB

	BLUE	WHITE	GREEN	RED
YDS:	430	375	348	331
PAR:	4	4	4	4
HDCP:	7	7	7	5

9

The finishing hole for the front is straightaway. The back tees are not only longer, but there is water to be carried as well. The marsh and a large bunker present themselves to the left.

Play the drive down the right side for safety. The length of the hole will become apparent on the approach.

The back third of the putting surface is flat, while the front third slopes to the front. If the green is missed, simply get the ball up and down in two to save the par. Finish the front on a good note!

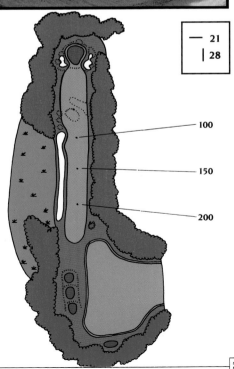

— 21
| 28

100

150

200

BEAR CREEK GOLF CLUB

10

	BLUE	WHITE	GREEN	RED
YDS:	390	367	347	336
PAR:	4	4	4	4
HDCP:	10	10	10	4

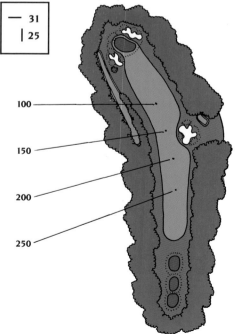

— 31
| 25

100

150

200

250

The tenth starts off with a bend to the left. It is a good idea to cut the corner by keeping the ball down the left side of the fairway.

A well hit shot will put the ball just past the corner for a straight approach at the flag. Bunkers, such as the one pictured, are found left and right of the green.

Play the second shot for the right side of the green, bringing it back toward the center with a draw. The deep bunkers situated on the left are best avoided.

BEAR CREEK GOLF CLUB

	BLUE	WHITE	GREEN	RED
YDS:	404	372	352	331
PAR:	4	4	4	4
HDCP:	8	8	8	12

11

The eleventh follows the form of the tenth. The drive on this hole, however, should be kept in the center of the fairway. A mighty drive down through the center of the fairway bunkers will put the ball in excellent position for the approach.

The green is surrounded by bunkers; accuracy is imperative. Gentle rolling of the putting surface increases the level of difficulty for the longer putts.

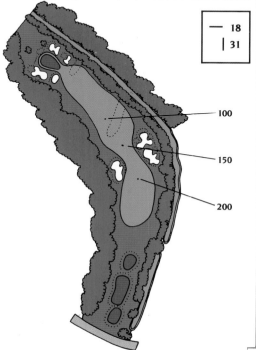

— 18
| 31

BEAR CREEK GOLF CLUB

12

	BLUE	WHITE	GREEN	RED
YDS:	191	154	143	134
PAR:	3	3	3	3
HDCP:	18	18	18	18

— 26
| 33

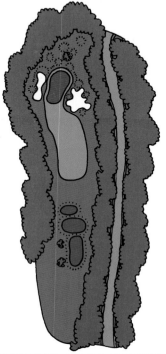

The twelfth is usually played with the wind blowing from behind. The big bunker located front right blocks visibilty of the green beyond. Pay attention to the actual yardage from the tee and choose your club accordingly.

The green slopes toward the front left corner and is tucked in among the bunkers. Once on the putting surface, the ball should fall on the first attempt.

BEAR CREEK GOLF CLUB

	BLUE	WHITE	GREEN	RED
YDS:	508	470	436	413
PAR:	5	5	5	5
HDCP:	6	6	6	8

13

The thirteenth may be reachable for the longer players, but accuracy will be a must on the second shot. A large pond ripples with anticipation for misguided shots.

A well hit drive, aimed just right of the fairway bunkers in the distance, is the most desirable shot off the tee.

The second shot should be restricted a little in order to stay short of the water.

Take a firm approach and hit directly at the flag to set up for a birdie possibility. The large green has an equally large mound in the center, creating a ridge that must to be crossed if the ball is hit to the wrong side of the green.

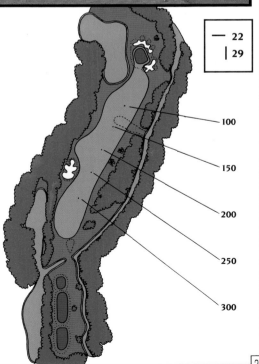

— 22
| 29

100

150

200

250

300

BEAR CREEK GOLF CLUB

14

	BLUE	WHITE	GREEN	RED
YDS:	166	155	124	114
PAR:	3	3	3	3
HDCP:	16	16	16	16

— 33
| 23

The wind will mean an added club or two on this hole when it's blowing against the player. The green is large and wedges towards the front, creating a small valley.

It is imperative to get the ball all the way to the putting surface. A ball that lands just on the front burm will probably be pulled back into the water! Make sure the shot is long enough.

Slippery sidehill downhill putts can be expected if the tee shot comes to rest above the hole.

BEAR CREEK GOLF CLUB

	BLUE	WHITE	GREEN	RED
YDS:	401	385	356	326
PAR:	4	4	4	4
HDCP:	2	2	2	10

15

This little hole is deceiving from the tee. The large bunkers on the left appear much closer than they actually are.

Aim the drive well right to keep clear of the trouble. The long approach is to an elevated green that slopes toward the front.

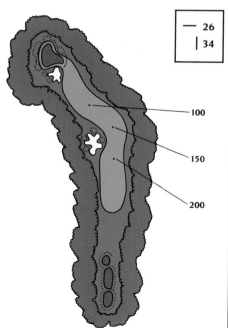

— 26
| 34

100

150

200

BEAR CREEK GOLF CLUB

16

	BLUE	WHITE	GREEN	RED
YDS:	371	361	336	309
PAR:	4	4	4	4
HDCP:	12	12	12	14

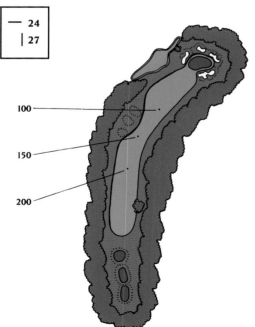

— 24
| 27

100
150
200

The shorter length of this hole will get the adrenalin pumping. The elevated tee gives the player a sense of invincibility as the ball is addressed. Par, even birdie, are as good as done!

Simply drive the ball down the center, hit the approach up to the cup and sink the putt!

Note that the green slopes rapidly from back to front. Some sidehill putts will seem impossible. Keep the ball below the hole on the approach.

BEAR CREEK GOLF CLUB

	BLUE	WHITE	GREEN	RED
YDS:	372	341	315	303
PAR:	4	4	4	4
HDCP:	14	14	14	6

17

The seventeenth tee shot will help fine tune the driver before the eighteenth. Length is not of great concern, but, keep the ball down the middle for best position on the approach.

The putting surface undulates from side to side. Be sure to get the ball close to the hole to avoid a long rolling putt. The finish is near, but it isn't over yet. This eighteenth is not excessively long. However, into the wind, it is not short! Bunkers on the right necessitate driving to the left.

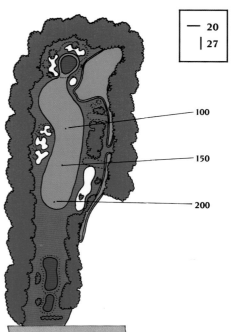

— 20
| 27

100

150

200

BEAR CREEK GOLF CLUB

18

	BLUE	WHITE	GREEN	RED
YDS:	502	492	462	422
PAR:	5	5	5	5
HDCP:	4	4	4	2

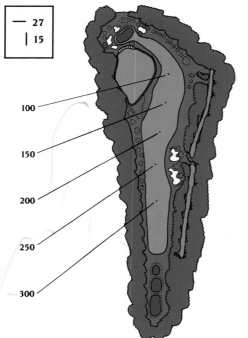

— 27
| 15

100

150

200

250

300

The second shot is the key. A well-placed shot to the right of the water is a must for a good angle to the pin.

Any attempts for the green from the left side of the fairway are futile, unless it is certain that enough club is being used.

The putting surface is small and flat. Impress the onlookers in the clubhouse and roll the first putt in! You have just gone head to head with the 'Bear'!

BEAR CREEK GOLF CLUB

Hilton Head Plantation
237 Whooping Crane Way
Hilton Head Island, SC 29926
803-681-2667
Private

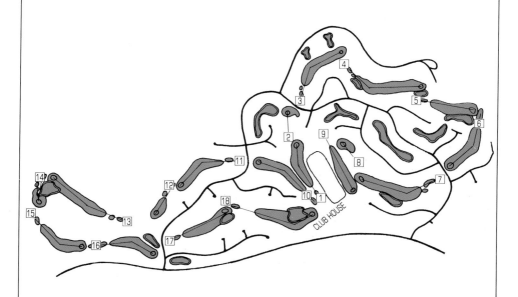

Head Professional: Bob Ward
Superintendent: Joe Robb
Designer: Rees Jones

Course	Rating	Slope
Gold	71.5	129
Blue	69.3	125
White	66.4	118
Red	70.5	116

HOLE	1	2	3	4	5	6	7	8	9	OUT	10	11	12	13	14	15	16	17	18	IN	TOTAL
BLUE	360	161	426	515	341	389	505	189	430	3316	390	404	191	508	166	401	371	372	502	3305	6621
WHITE	326	134	394	485	334	357	478	165	375	3048	367	372	154	470	155	385	361	341	492	3097	6145
GREEN	314	107	369	457	303	341	436	124	348	2799	347	352	143	436	124	356	336	315	462	2871	5670
HDCP	15	17	1	5	11	9	3	13	7		10	8	18	6	16	2	12	14	4		
PAR	4	3	4	5	4	4	5	3	4	36	4	4	3	5	3	4	4	4	5	36	72
RED	310	102	338	427	292	322	410	104	331	2636	336	331	134	413	114	326	309	303	422	2688	2636
HDCP	11	17	1	3	13	9	7	15	5		4	12	18	8	16	10	14	6	2		

COUNTRY CLUB of HILTON HEAD

The Course

Rees Jones designed this distinctive Hilton Head Island golf course. The course is situated at the furthest point from Hilton Head Plantation's main gate. In fact, it's right next to the back gate! This location is ideal for a layout that incorporates the rolling features of the land with scenic intercoastal views. The course wanders from open expanses to deep within wooded lands and out again. As soon as the round begins, the golfer will become aware of the abundant mounding that sets the tone for a layout from the first hole right through to the final putt on eighteen.

Accuracy is a must off the first tee. The drive should split the center of the fairway and keep clear of fairway bunkers on either side. The front side can be considered a preparation nine for the back side. The greens, however, present a true test of ones putting skills from very beginning. The par 5 sixth hole is the shortest par 5 at 491 yards. This course is played best when you take advantage of such opportunities. Length really does not become a factor until the ninth hole, a par 4 at 433 yards.

On the tenth hole, the course proclaims that it — not you — is master. With its 423-yard length and narrow landing area, the tenth is difficult enough. However, throw in a green bordered by bunkers on its left and water to the right, and the result is a very demanding first hole for the back side. The holes follow through to an intercoastal view on the twelfth, a boardwalk journey on the fourteenth, and finally finish up with a long par 5 eighteenth which features the only bowl-like green in the area.

COUNTRY CLUB of HILTON HEAD

1

	GOLD	BLUE	WHITE	RED
YDS:	398	365	335	310
PAR:	4	4	4	4
HDCP:	14	14	14	11

The notorious ''dew scrapers'' are found only very early in the morning. These unique and rare creatures are usually found with wet shoes and wide open eyes. Their tracks can be found criss-crossing fairways.

An early Rees Jones is the introduction to this course, making it a true test of a golfer's ability. Two sand bunkers right, along with sand bunker and grass bunkers left, define the boundaries of this first fairway. The drive must be hit straight down the middle. Any deviation left or right will make the approach more difficult.

The second shot is to a slightly elevated green. Three bunkers front the putting surface. Mounding is found beyond. A slight slope in the green will test the credentials of the putter.

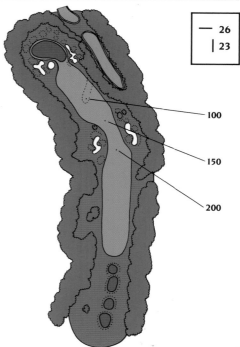

— 26
| 23

100

150

200

COUNTRY CLUB of HILTON HEAD

2

	GOLD	BLUE	WHITE	RED
YDS:	413	393	364	336
PAR:	4	4	4	4
HDCP:	6	6	6	5

— 18
| 24

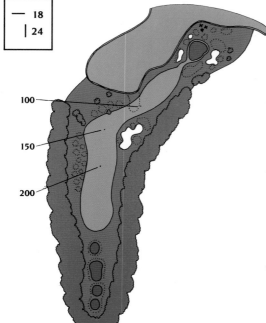

100

150

200

The second hole is a bit less demanding from the tee. The approach shot, however, requires a solid shot to the green — ignoring the water and bunkers that fill the view.

Play the drive straight away. Mounding left and a lone bunker to the right will foil the errant tee shot. From the center of the fairway the approach can be simple.

About 150 yards to the green should be left after the drive. A crisp iron shot to the center of the green will certainly guarantee a par. Be advised that the putting surface will seem very small and difficult to hit from the fairway. Simply put a good move on the ball, and watch it land softly on the green.

COUNTRY CLUB of HILTON HEAD

	GOLD	BLUE	WHITE	RED	3
YDS:	166	156	130	94	
PAR:	3	3	3	3	
HDCP:	18	18	18	17	

The first taste of a par 3 on this golf course includes a little water. It is of the upmost importance to carry the water on the tee shot. Be sure to not only clear the water, but also get the ball past the front of the green. Any shots shy of the putting surface have a good chance of rolling back down the slope, ending up wet.

The putting surface is backed by bunkers, catching the over-zealous tee shots. Once on the short grass, putts should fall on the first attempt.

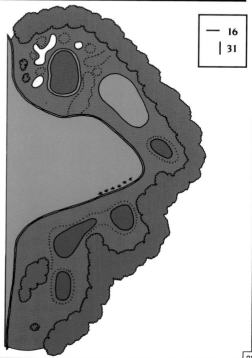

—	16
|	31

COUNTRY CLUB of HILTON HEAD

4

	GOLD	BLUE	WHITE	RED
YDS:	431	407	384	364
PAR:	4	4	4	4
HDCP:	2	2	2	7

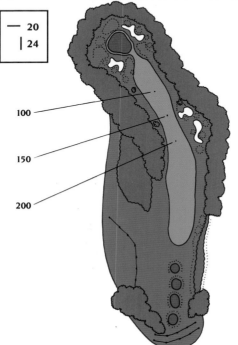

— 20

| 24

100

150

200

Accuracy off the tee is advised. The slight dogleg left will require a drive past the corner in order to see the green. Fairway bunkers to the right are a good target from the tee. Play the drive just left of the bunkers.

The approach is to an elevated green. With the fairway wedged in among the trees, it is important to know that the winds are stronger above the tree line. If the second shot is to be played high, note the wind direction and play accordingly.

The putting surface slopes ever so slightly toward the front. Similar to the last hole, the putts should drop quickly. Actually the greens are fairly flat on every hole. You can't blame the putter for misses on this course.

COUNTRY CLUB of HILTON HEAD

	GOLD	BLUE	WHITE	RED
YDS:	358	338	326	301
PAR:	4	4	4	4
HDCP:	8	8	8	3

5

Although the hole is not that long and the fairway is straight and wide, there is a small water hazard to be crossed on the approach. Birdies, however, are not out of the question.

A drive down the left middle of the fairway will set up a good position for the approach. Be careful! The fairway bunkers along the left are perilously close to off the tee.

The putting surface is receptive to well-hit approach shots. Sloping slightly toward the front, the green provides a great target that should be taken advantage of. The pros call it throwing darts when an approach is as easy as this one.

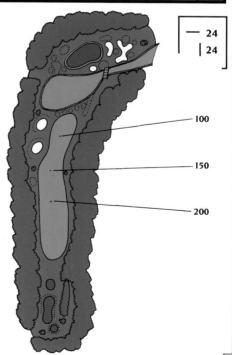

COUNTRY CLUB of HILTON HEAD

6

	GOLD	BLUE	WHITE	RED
YDS:	491	467	461	405
PAR:	5	5	5	5
HDCP:	12	12	12	9

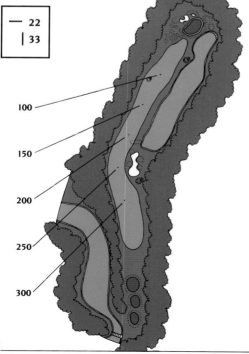

Two good knocks can get you to this green. (That's for the longer players.) The safe way to play this hole is to hit the drive along the left side of the fairway, followed by a second shot, again down the left side. A short approach to the green should come to rest inches from the cup. Birdie.

The riskier route is to crunch the drive along the right side of the fairway, accented with a slight fade. The second shot will then be from about 220 yards from the green. A solid accurate shot will sail onto the putting surface. Two putts later, the birdie can be marked down on the scorecard.

COUNTRY CLUB of HILTON HEAD

	GOLD	BLUE	WHITE	RED
YDS:	171	143	133	103
PAR:	3	3	3	3
HDCP:	16	16	16	15

There is not as much water as the third hole. However, this par 3 can be just as difficult. The pines tighten the approach path to the green. Winds can surprise a lofted shot.

Attention must be focused on the center of the green. Don't be preoccupied with the bunkers surrounding the putting surface. Play one shot at a time and hit this tee shot to the green. A par on this hole is as good as birdies on others.

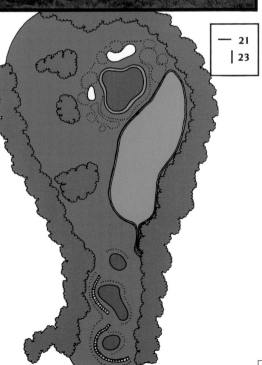

— 21
| 23

COUNTRY CLUB of HILTON HEAD

8

	GOLD	BLUE	WHITE	RED
YDS:	518	496	487	460
PAR:	5	5	5	5
HDCP:	10	10	10	1

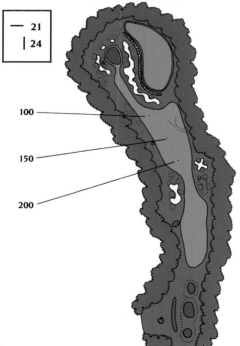

— 21

| 24

100

150

200

It would seem that a par 4 should follow the last hole. Not so on this course. Mr. Jones does not let the golfer off so easily. Three good shots are a must in order to get the ball onto the green in regulation.

The drive should be hit down the right side of the fairway, keeping clear of the bunker to the left. This large bunker will quickly dash hopes of achieving birdie.

The second shot must be placed on the left side of the fairway. A long bunker sweeps in from the right side, leaving a narrow path of fairway to the green.

COUNTRY CLUB of HILTON HEAD

	GOLD	BLUE	WHITE	RED	
YDS:	433	410	398	372	**9**
PAR:	4	4	4	4	
HDCP:	4	4	4	13	

The path to the clubhouse is long and difficult. Many good rounds can be ruined on this hole if care is not taken to play smart. Three bunkers lie in the distance from the tee — all reachable. Precision off the tee will help keep the ball in the short grass.

From the fairway, the approach can be expected to be long. A well-hit shot is required to get the ball up onto the putting surface.

The green is hidden by gentle mounding. Bunkers are placed strategically among the mounds. A par on this hole will most certainly keep your game alive for the back nine.

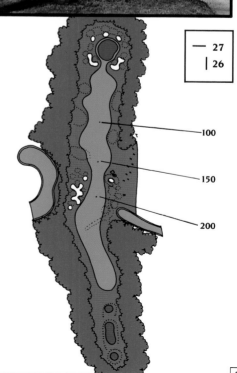

— 27
| 26

100

150

200

10	GOLD	BLUE	WHITE	RED
YDS:	423	396	388	360
PAR:	4	4	4	4
HDCP:	1	1	1	2

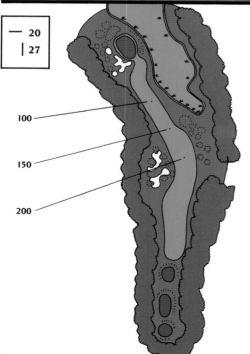

— 20
| 27

100

150

200

The back side starts off with a hole that requires full concentration. It may not be necessary to use the driver. A fairway wood or even a long iron will do the job just fine. Bunkers and trees along the left side extend outward into the fairway, blocking out any shots from that side.

COUNTRY CLUB of HILTON HEAD

	GOLD	BLUE	WHITE	RED
YDS:	184	178	151	115
PAR:	3	3	3	3
HDCP:	15	15	15	16

11

A medium-length par 3, this eleventh hole demands an accurate tee shot. The green slopes slightly from back to front. The bunker to the left will grab those who try to play too safe. Two bunkers right should be out of play, but, a pushed shot may find them.

The putting surface may yield a birdie if the ball has landed near the hole.

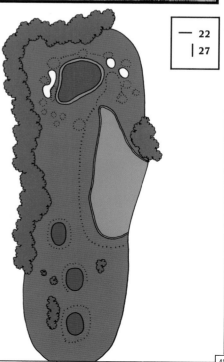

— 22
| 27

COUNTRY CLUB of HILTON HEAD

12

	GOLD	BLUE	WHITE	RED
YDS:	575	540	511	480
PAR:	5	5	5	5
HDCP:	9	9	9	10

If it is raining during your round and flooding is imminent, run for the high ground. Actually this twelfth hole is the highest point on Hilton Head Island at 28.24 feet above sea level.

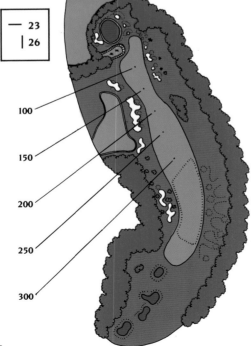

— 23
| 26

100
150
200
250
300

The elevated teeing area is just a steppingstone to the elevated fairway. The fairway is so high, in fact, that it's actually the highest point of Hilton Head Island. If you want to reach the green in three shots, they'll have to be good, long ones.

This hole should be played right down the middle of the fairway. Be careful to keep the ball in the center of the fairway in order to avoid having it careen left or right of the plateau fairway.

The second shot should be directed down the middle of the fairway, staying clear of the bunkers left and right.

The third shot will be from about 120 yards. The ocean is in view beyond the trees. Winds will most likely be picking up. A strong approach shot is a must. Note the marsh that creeps in from the left, protecting the front of the green.

	GOLD	BLUE	WHITE	RED
YDS:	438	415	401	393
PAR:	4	4	4	4
HDCP:	5	5	5	8

Longer hitters may be able to cut the corner on this par 4. The rest of us, however, will play a safer drive down the right middle of the fairway. Aiming to the right of the farthest visible fairway bunker will set up for the approach.

The approach is to a slightly elevated green well protected by bunkers. The putting surface slopes toward the front. An approach that lands any-where near the hole will be easily knocked into the cup on the first try.

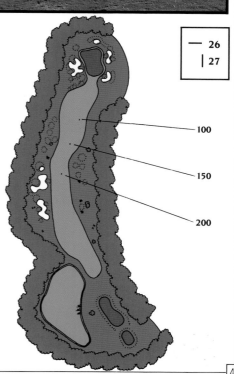

— 26
| 27

100

150

200

COUNTRY CLUB of HILTON HEAD

14

	GOLD	BLUE	WHITE	RED
YDS:	185	160	152	70
PAR:	3	3	3	3
HDCP:	13	13	13	18

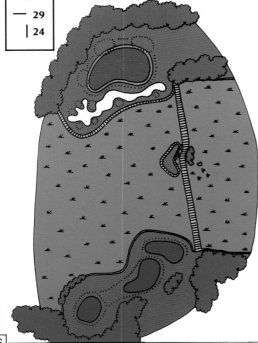

— 29
| 24

The marsh comes into full view on this hole. Swirling winds will add difficulty to the tee shot. The elevated green is guarded by a large bunker. It is vital to hit the ball long enough to clear the hazards. But don't hit too long; the backside of the green slopes into the woods.

The putting surface is divided in half by a ridge running front to back. Try to keep the ball on the same side as the pin in order to avoid a long, tricky putt.

COUNTRY CLUB of HILTON HEAD

	GOLD	BLUE	WHITE	RED
YDS:	378	358	351	328
PAR:	4	4	4	4
HDCP:	11	11	11	6

15

The fifteenth is a fairly short dogleg right. The fairway bunkers left are within driving distance. You have to work at it to get the ball into the water to the right, with a big push or slice, for instance.

Position off the tee is more important than length. A fairway wood or long iron is all that is required. The best position for the approach is slightly right of center fairway.

A second shot of approximately 150 yards is to an elevated green. The gentle rolling of the fairway makes the green appear farther away and smaller than it actually is. Two bunkers on either side will catch errant shots. The putting surface slopes toward the front of the green.

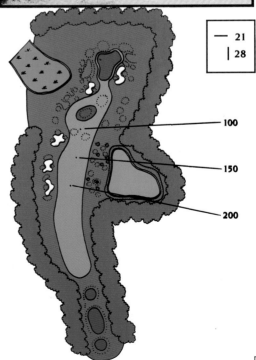

— 21
| 28

100

150

200

	GOLD	BLUE	WHITE	RED
YDS:	376	373	358	342
PAR:	4	4	4	4
HDCP:	7	7	7	4

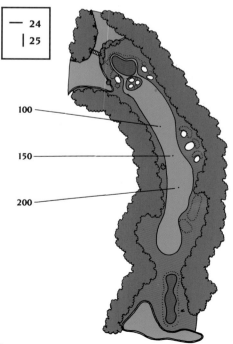

— 24
| 25

100

150

200

The sixteenth lets you to relax a bit. The fairway slopes slowly up away from the tee. The drive will sail over a ridge down into the center of the fairway, leaving about 160 yards to the green. The approach must be played to the center of the green, evading the bunkers which surround the green. The green slopes from the back left to the front right.

Two well-thought-out shots should be able to get the ball up onto the green and close to the hole. Concentration with the putter may help score a birdie.

COUNTRY CLUB of HILTON HEAD

	GOLD	BLUE	WHITE	RED	**17**
YDS:	402	392	286	273	
PAR:	4	4	4	4	
HDCP:	17	17	17	14	

The view from the back tees may cause concern about the drive. A straight and long drive is vital in order to reach the green in regulation. Any deviation offline may snag a branch and deflect the ball into trouble. Bunkers along the right side of the fairway should be avoided at all costs, otherwise deep sand will make the par very difficult to achieve.

The approach is to an elevated green which slants toward the front. Three more bunkers lie in wait for the errant shot. Keeping the ball below the hole will allow for an easier uphill putt.

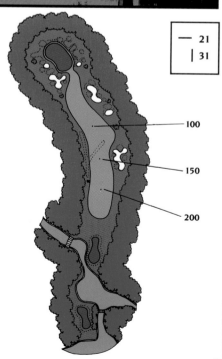

COUNTRY CLUB of HILTON HEAD

18

	GOLD	BLUE	WHITE	RED
YDS:	579	556	546	507
PAR:	5	5	5	5
HDCP:	3	3	3	12

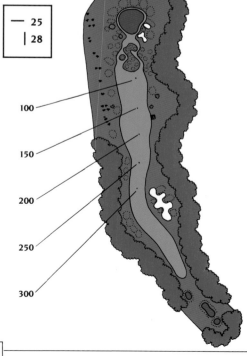

— 25
| 28

100

150

200

250

300

Mr. Jones has stretched this last hole out just enough to make it a very worthy finale. A tailwind can be very helpful here. One lone fairway bunker along the right side will pursuade you to drive toward the left. Once beyond that bunker, the fairway opens up, allowing for tensions to abate. Three well-hit shots will get the ball up to the green, setting up for the birdie.

From the left side of the fairway, the second shot should be played down the left side. Be careful not to pull this shot. Out of bounds borders on the left. A medium approach shot should be left to the green.

Mounding in front gives the illusion that the green is farther away than it actually is. Bunkers left and right keep the game interesting. The large mounding beyond the green will keep the longer shots close. A par is nice, but a birdie would finish the day with style.

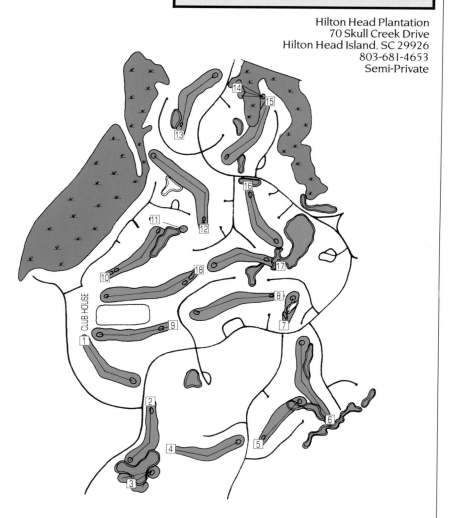

COUNTRY CLUB of HILTON HEAD

Hilton Head Plantation
70 Skull Creek Drive
Hilton Head Island, SC 29926
803-681-4653
Semi-Private

CLUB HOUSE

Course	Rating	Slope
Gold	73.6	132
Blue	71.7	128
White	70.0	124
Red	72.8	126

Head Professional: Bob Thomas
Superintendent: Cail Callison
Designer: Rees Jones
Teaching Professional: Skip Malek

HOLE	1	2	3	4	5	6	7	8	9	OUT	10	11	12	13	14	15	16	17	18	IN	TOTAL
GOLD	398	413	166	431	358	491	171	518	433	3379	423	184	575	438	185	378	376	402	579	3540	6919
BLUE	365	393	156	407	338	467	143	496	410	3175	396	178	540	415	160	358	373	392	556	3368	6543
WHITE	335	364	130	384	326	461	133	487	398	3018	388	151	511	401	152	351	358	286	546	3144	6162
HDCP	14	6	18	2	8	12	16	10	4		1	15	9	5	13	11	7	17	3		
PAR	4	4	3	4	4	5	3	5	4	36	4	3	5	4	3	4	4	4	5	36	72
RED	310	336	94	364	301	405	103	460	372	2745	360	115	480	393	70	328	342	273	507	2868	5613
HDCP	11	5	17	7	3	9	15	1	13		2	16	10	8	18	6	4	14	12		

DOLPHIN HEAD GOLF COURSE

The Course

Located in Hilton Head Plantaion, Dolphin Head Golf Club is the northernmost golf course on Hilton Head Island. Designed in 1974 by Gary Player and Ron Kirby, it is definitely a course to be reckoned with. At just under 6600 yards, it's not long — but then again, it's not short either. Rolling fairways are bordered by large, menacing pines. Greens are level and elevated, varying from hole to hole. Player and Kirby have done an excellent job in designing the course so that it is interesting from start to finish — its character changing as the round progresses.

Nestled among the pines, the golf course actually ventures into the woodlands for the starting nine. The first hole begins boldly with a tough, dogleg par 5. The sloping green quickly tests your skills with the putter. The second and third holes are short par 4's, but the rolling fairways make for difficult approach shots. The front finishes as it had started; with a solid par 5 demanding a final approach over a good sized pond. The many doglegs and water hazards on the front nine reveal the challenges yet to come.

The turn to the back nine takes the golfer out toward the ocean. This nine, a bit longer than the front, confirms Dolphin Head's worthiness. The fourteenth swings out to a seaside view. Up to the eighteenth the golfer is not given a choice of how to play each hole. But here one is offered the alternative of taking just a little more risk. Keep it left and play it safe, or go right and get to the par 5 in two!

DOLPHIN HEAD GOLF CLUB

	BLUE	WHITE	GOLD	RED	**1**
YDS:	514	468	456	435	
PAR:	5	5	5	5	
HDCP:	9	9	9	5	

Dolphin Head starts off with a good par 5. Right from the start you are aware that this course is serious. Trees line the right side of the fairway while the left opens up a bit. The tee shot must be played down the left middle of the fairway. The second shot follows down the middle. The longer hitters may be able to reach this green in two, although care must be taken to avoid the bunkers right and left of the putting surface.

The green slopes toward the front from a flat area on the back right. Care is of the essence to keep the ball short of the hole for an uphill putt to the cup. Slippery downhill putts can be expected if the approach is too long.

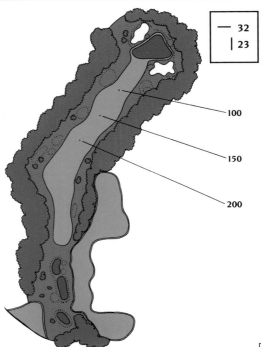

— 32
| 23

100

150

200

DOLPHIN HEAD GOLF CLUB

2

	BLUE	WHITE	GOLD	RED
YDS:	340	326	326	297
PAR:	4	4	4	4
HDCP:	11	11	11	9

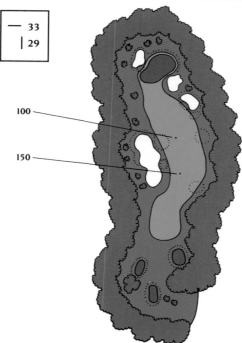

— 33
| 29

100

150

Under 400 yards, this second hole will get the adrenalin pumping. Accuracy is a must to keep the drive down the left middle of the fairway, avoiding the fairway bunker on the right. The driver may cause trouble; back down to a fairway wood or long iron off the tee. The fairway rolls gently toward the green, so an approach shot may not be from a flat lie. Pin placement can determine whether this is a simple birdie hole or one that requires work for the par. A smooth swing should nestle the ball inches away from the cup when placed up front. Go for the center of the putting surface when the pin is in the back right corner.

Similar to the second, this third hole has a very tight landing area. The near bunker on the left has claimed many mishit tee shots. The next bunker on the right means you need a somewhat longer drive to be in play. A conservative drive along the right middle of the fairway is ideal positioning.

The approach is to a green sloping slightly to the left. Gary Player has assured the golfer that he is command as the second shot will most likely be played from a sidehill lie. What Player has not accounted for is the crisp iron shot that falls inches away from the hole. Tap in the putt and pencil in the 3 on your scorecard!

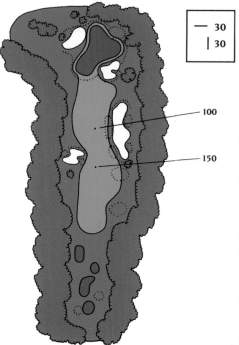

— 30

| 30

100

150

DOLPHIN HEAD GOLF CLUB

4		BLUE	WHITE	GOLD	RED
	YDS:	174	151	133	117
	PAR:	3	3	3	3
	HDCP:	15	15	15	15

— 37
| 35

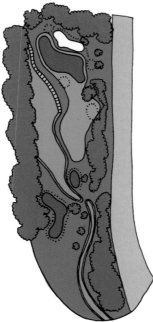

This rather short par 4 can surprise those who overestimate it. A well-hit tee shot may be pulled off course by winds blowing just above the tree line. Play the shot slightly to the right, bringing it back gently to the left and keeping the ball over dry land as long as possible. Be carefull not to allow the ball to veer too much left.

Note that the green is positioned close to the water's edge. Any shots just slightly mishit will most likely end up wet.

DOLPHIN HEAD GOLF CLUB				
	BLUE	WHITE	GOLD	RED
YDS:	361	342	321	273
PAR:	4	4	4	4
HDCP:	7	7	7	13

5

From the tee box, the view reveals a dogleg that turns rapidly to the right. A slight dip just off the tee box rises back up at the corner of the dogleg. The rolling fairway may cause uncertainty at the tee. Simply play the drive down the left center of the fairway and let the ball bounce along without concern. The main concern is to keep the ball left of both the bunker and the ditch along the right side. The approach may be from an uneven lie. The green slopes abruptly from back to front. Try to position the second shot below the hole, leaving a fairly easy uphill putt.

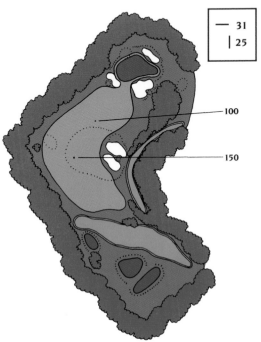

— 31
| 25

100

150

DOLPHIN HEAD GOLF CLUB

6

	BLUE	WHITE	GOLD	RED
YDS:	433	410	351	342
PAR:	4	4	4	4
HDCP:	1	1	1	3

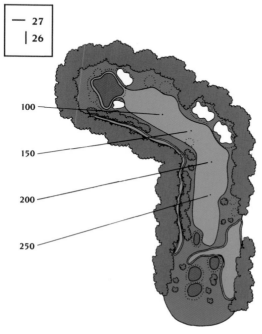

Hopefully the last few par 4's have not spoiled you. Where those holes required accuracy and finesse, this sixth hole demands the long game. The dogleg left will cause a few to think the hole can be shortened by cutting the corner. Unfortunately, that is not the case. A long drive down the middle is a must in order to get home in two. If that is not possible, simply play the hole as a par 5 — and birdie it!

The elevated green is surrounded by bunkers. Any deviations may end in the sand. An approach shot aimed for the center of the green is advised. A bogey here is a good score.

DOLPHIN HEAD GOLF CLUB

	BLUE	WHITE	GOLD	RED	7
YDS:	201	178	151	143	
PAR:	3	3	3	3	
HDCP:	17	17	17	17	

A bit longer than the fourth hole, this par 3 should not cause any problems. Straight and simple, the tee shot should be played with enough club. The two bunkers fronting the green offer only a minimal gap between them. The large putting surface slopes toward the front, posing a challenge to the birdie putter.

— 32
| 25

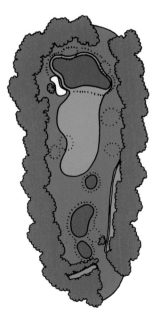

DOLPHIN HEAD GOLF CLUB

8

	BLUE	WHITE	GOLD	RED
YDS:	400	380	347	339
PAR:	4	4	4	4
HDCP:	3	3	3	7

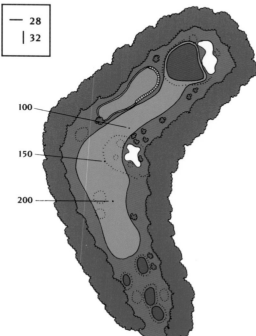

The right side of the fairway portends nothing but disaster. The lone tree just off the tee can grab any shots that venture too close. The drive that sets sail over the tree may find the fairway bunker. Obviously, the shot to play off the tee is down the left side. Too far left, however, will leave a long approach into the green. A long drive straight down the middle may bound happlessly into the water.

The approach is played into a green that, curiously, slopes drastically to the left. Caution should be observed to keep the second shot from homing into the water. Tricky putts can be made when the ball is long and right of the hole. One bunker beyond the green will catch those who hit the approach too long.

	BLUE	WHITE	GOLD	RED
YDS:	516	493	459	453
PAR:	5	5	5	5
HDCP:	5	5	5	1

9

The pond in front of the green may discourage those who would like the green to be reachable in two strokes. However, with the right conditions, this is not impossible! The rest of us should play the drive safely down the center of the fairway. A second shot to the left side will set up for a good angle on the approach.

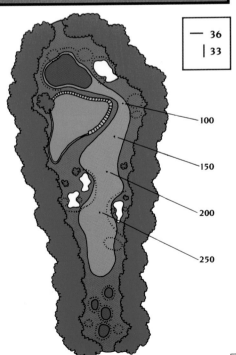

— 36
| 33

100

150

200

250

DOLPHIN HEAD GOLF CLUB

10

	BLUE	WHITE	GOLD	RED
YDS:	371	350	293	285
PAR:	4	4	4	4
HDCP:	8	8	8	12

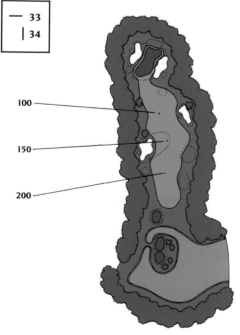

The drive must pass the left fairway bunker in order to have the green in sight for the second shot. Aim the tee shot down the middle, straight for the fairway bunkers on the outside of the dogleg. The approach is to a slightly elevated green, cut in among the pines. The putting surface slopes toward the front left. Keeping the ball short and below the hole will insure a fairly easy uphill putt. Starting the back side off with a par sets the tone for some good scoring yet to come.

DOLPHIN HEAD GOLF CLUB

	BLUE	WHITE	GOLD	RED
YDS:	391	374	364	332
PAR:	4	4	4	4
HDCP:	6	6	6	6

11

Gary Player has placed a bunker along the right side of the fairway to discourage the shortcut on this dogleg right. There is no real benefit in playing along the right side, so, instead, play smart and hit the drive down the left center. This will place the ball in an ideal position for the approach.

The large putting surface is cut diagonally back to the right. Length can be added to the hole with a pin placement in the back right corner. The slowly rolling surface adds dimension to the longer putts. Careful attention to the putter will guarantee no more than a two putt.

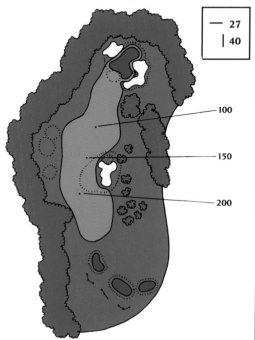

— 27

| 40

100

150

200

DOLPHIN HEAD GOLF CLUB

12

	BLUE	WHITE	GOLD	RED
YDS:	214	192	152	145
PAR:	3	3	3	3
HDCP:	14	14	14	18

— 29
| 36

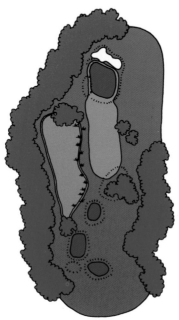

The length of the hole is not the only test of this par 3. The hole is cut tightly in among the trees. Any stray offline will surely be grabbed by a branch. A longer club may have to be used to get to the flag. The surface slopes quickly to the front; some tricky putts may be encountered.

DOLPHIN HEAD GOLF CLUB

	BLUE	WHITE	GOLD	RED
YDS:	524	505	468	460
PAR:	5	5	5	5
HDCP:	4	4	4	4

13

The thirteenth allows for a big driving area. The fairway zigs left, then zags right up near the green. Fairway bunkers along the right side should be out of play — unless a dreadful slice is hit off the tee. A drive down the left side will most likely be blocked for the second shot. The middle of the fairway is the best position. The second shot should be played slightly down the left, opening up the green for a clear approach. The putting surface slopes back to front, with a bunker fronting the left side.

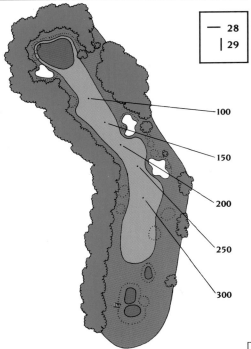

— 28
| 29

100

150

200

250

300

DOLPHIN HEAD GOLF CLUB

14

	BLUE	WHITE	GOLD	RED
YDS:	341	330	332	272
PAR:	4	4	4	4
HDCP:	18	18	18	14

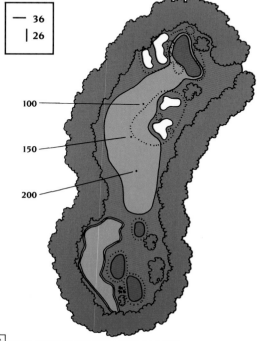

Rated as the easiest hole on the course, that is if it is played correctly! A beautiful view of Port Royal Sound comes into sight from the corner of the dogleg. A good way of getting to this vantage point is to aim the drive down the left side of the fairway; incidentally, this is also the best route to the green. Bunkers and trees along the right block out most shots that are played from the right.

The approach shot should be hit with enough club to get the ball all the way to the flag. The gusty winds from the ocean can push a seemingly well-hit shot offline. By using enough club and accounting for the breeze, you can keep the green within reach. Pin placements on the left side are difficult to get to. Two bunkers short and right of the putting surface can endanger the second shot. Note the shortness of the wide green. Accuracy is a must to keep the ball on the green.

DOLPHIN HEAD GOLF CLUB

	BLUE	WHITE	GOLD	RED
YDS:	435	396	386	320
PAR:	4	4	4	4
HDCP:	2	2	2	8

15

What the fourteenth lacked in length, the fifteenth makes up for. A careful drive along the left side of the fairway will keep well clear of the bunker to the right. With or without a headwind, a long approach shot to this green should be anticipated. Water along the left should not come into play. However, it does make its presence known.

The approach shot is to an elevated green which slopes radically from back to front. Bunkers left and right also add some difficulty to the par. Play conservatively. Even a bogey on this hole is a good score.

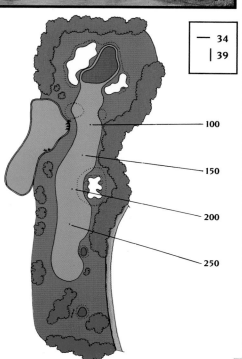

— 34
| 39

— 100

— 150

— 200

— 250

DOLPHIN HEAD GOLF CLUB

16

	BLUE	WHITE	GOLD	RED
YDS:	357	341	333	300
PAR:	4	4	4	4
HDCP:	10	10	10	10

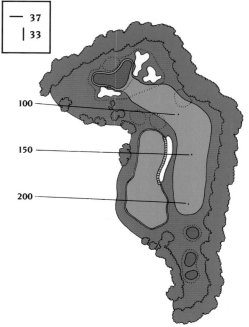

— 37
| 33

100

150

200

The sixteenth incorporates the pond from the fifteenth. The dogleg, bending to the left, requires a drive down the right middle of the fairway, leaving a moderate approach to the green.

A bunker short right winds curiously around to the right, while a bunker left sits just waiting for a visitor. The approach should be played right to the flag; the putting surface is tough to get to. Mounding beyond and a slight slope toward the front produces a rolling green.

DOLPHIN HEAD GOLF CLUB

	BLUE	WHITE	GOLD	RED
YDS:	182	165	157	143
PAR:	4	4	4	4
HDCP:	16	16	16	16

17

Straight away — this seventeenth, par 3, is easier than it looks. Water to the right and bunkers to the left may catch a few errant shots. A solid tee shot should be aimed to the left side of the green and allowed to move right. Pay attention to the wind that blows above the tree line. A birdie on this hole should close the lid on the competition.

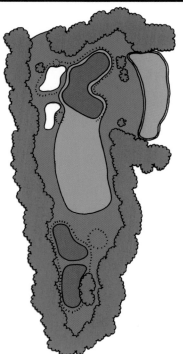

— 31
| 45

DOLPHIN HEAD GOLF CLUB

18

	BLUE	WHITE	GOLD	RED
YDS:	490	476	462	421
PAR:	5	5	5	5
HDCP:	12	12	12	2

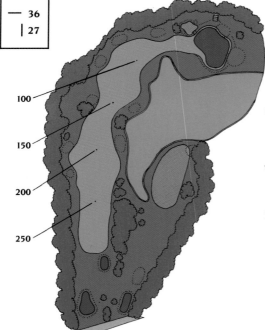

— 36

| 27

100

150

200

250

This finishing hole gives the player a choice: Either play conservatively down the left, or go for the green in two by playing to the right fairway.

Playing safe is accomplished by hitting the drive down the left middle of the fairway. Water sneaks in from the right and can lure those who play too far to the right. The second shot should also be hit down the left side, keeping well clear of the water to the right and setting up a good angle for the approach. The dogleg on this hole is not apparent until the final 150 yards. Almost at 90 degrees, the fairway turns sharply to the right, up to the green. The third shot should be played from around 100 yards out and should be hit solidly to the hole. Ending up short and/or right will most likely be wet.

DOLPHIN HEAD GOLF CLUB

Hilton Head Plantation
P.O. Box 21764
Hilton Head Island, SC 29925
803-681-2606
Private

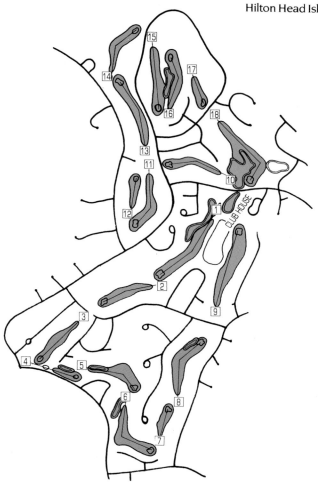

Head Professional: Burrell Williams
Superintendent: Larry Howz
Designers: Gary Player & Ron Kirby

Course	Rating	Slope
Blue	71.5	127
White	70.3	125
Gold	66.2	112
Red	71.8	120

HOLE	1	2	3	4	5	6	7	8	9	OUT	10	11	12	13	14	15	16	17	18	IN	TOTAL
BLUE	514	340	354	174	361	433	201	400	516	3293	371	391	214	524	341	435	357	182	490	3305	6598
WHITE	468	326	321	151	342	410	178	380	493	3069	350	374	192	505	330	396	341	165	476	3129	6198
GOLD	456	326	321	133	321	351	151	347	459	2865	293	364	152	468	332	386	333	157	462	2947	5812
HDCP	9	11	13	15	7	1	17	3	5		8	6	14	4	18	2	10	16	12		
PAR	5	4	4	3	4	4	3	4	5	36	4	4	3	5	4	4	4	3	5	36	72
RED	435	297	281	117	273	342	143	339	453	2680	285	332	145	460	272	320	300	143	421	2678	5358
HDCP	5	9	11	15	13	3	17	7	1		12	6	18	4	14	8	10	16	2		

OYSTER REEF GOLF CLUB

The Course

Opened for play in 1982, this Rees Jones golf course quickly became known as a formidable test of golfing ability. In 1983, Oyster Reef was named one of the top 25 new courses in America. Newly aquired by its members in the fall of 1990, the course has now undergone a few modifications. The biggest physical change is the increase of 66 yards to the Championship course, topping the total yardage at 7027 yards. As of this printing date, Oyster Reef is the longest course on the island. Couple that with the rolling fairways and undulating greens of a Rees Jones-designed golf course, and the result is one of the most challenging courses on the island.

The first hole starts off fairly simple — slight dogleg right, par 4. The first green is small and consistent with what is to be expected for the remainder of the round. The second hole is where the course gets serious. A well-placed drive should find the fairway just right of large fairway bunkers. From the tee shot looking toward the hole, the view is filled with mounding; navigation to the hole requires a bit of skill and a little luck. The par 3, sixth hole, leads out towards Port Royal Sound for a fantastic sight! The ninth seems to combine all of Rees Jones's trademarks in one hole — fairway bunkers, doglegs, severe mounding and an elevated undulating green.

The back side is as tough as the front. The yardage even stretches to a bit longer than the front. The two finishing par 4's, seventeen and eighteen, are both over 450 yards!

OYSTER REEF GOLF CLUB

	GOLD	BLUE	WHITE	RED
YDS:	391	364	342	267
PAR:	4	4	4	4
HDCP:	13	13	13	11

1

It will soon become apparent that Rees Jones has designed Oyster Reef as a course in which accuracy, not length, is a necessity for a good score. This first hole demonstrates that fact. Positioning off the tee is a must to set up the approach shot. A well-hit drive should end up along the left middle of the fairway — just opening up the angle to the green.

The green is long, so club selection is vital for the accurate approach. Gentle sloping from right to left adds difficulty to the longer putts.

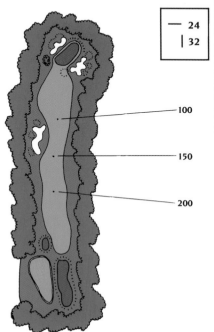

— 24
| 32

100

150

200

OYSTER REEF GOLF CLUB

2

	GOLD	BLUE	WHITE	RED
YDS:	514	480	463	427
PAR:	5	5	5	5
HDCP:	9	9	9	1

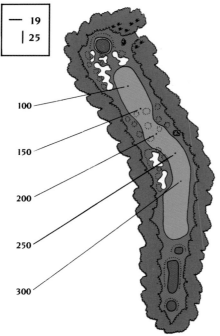

Positioning is vital on this second hole. Play the drive down the right side of the fairway. This par 5, although the longer hitters may be able to reach in two, is best played conservatively. The second shot should follow down the center, keeping well clear of the bunker along the left.

The approach is to an elevated green which is well protected by bunkers. Short is sandy; be sure to use enough club to get the ball to the hole. The relatively small putting surface is flat and will yield many one putts. It's a good hole to birdie!

OYSTER REEF GOLF CLUB

	GOLD	BLUE	WHITE	RED	
YDS:	175	168	145	118	**3**
PAR:	3	3	3	3	
HDCP:	17	17	17	17	

Starting here, Rees Jones has relaxed his level of difficulty for a few holes. Take advantage of the opportunity and play these next three holes smart. Birdies are a real possibility.

Bunkers cover the four corners of the green. Play the tee shot for the flagstick. The large putting surface can give the illusion that the hole is closer than it actually is. Pay special attention to the pin placement and choose your club accordingly.

The putting surface slopes toward the front, so some difficult putts can be expected if the ball is hit past the hole. When below the hole, the uphill putt is easier to knock into the cup.

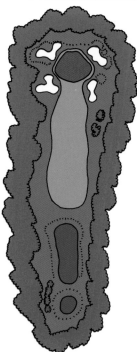

— 26
| 28

OYSTER REEF GOLF CLUB

	GOLD	BLUE	WHITE	RED
YDS:	375	364	341	317
PAR:	4	4	4	4
HDCP:	5	5	5	9

4

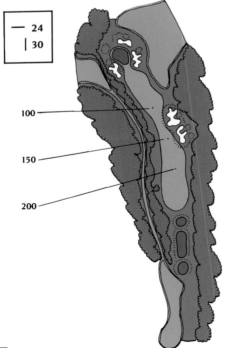

— 24
| 30

100

150

200

This fourth hole can be very short and easy to birdy. Sometimes, however, the ball does not fly as planned, and the hole becomes quite difficult. Accuracy off the tee is a must. The trees along the left side come in toward the fairway, blocking out the left side. As if that were not enough, the bunkers along the right add a bit of intimidation to the drive.

Ignore the problem areas and simply drive the ball down the right center of the fairway — setting up the perfect angle for the approach. The perfect drive should come to rest just beyond the prominent tree along the left, leaving an approach of approximately 130 yards.

The elevated green is well bunkered, requiring a controlled approach. Once on the putting surface, your putts should fall easily.

OYSTER REEF GOLF CLUB

	GOLD	BLUE	WHITE	RED
YDS:	455	397	372	326
PAR:	4	4	4	4
HDCP:	3	3	3	7

5

This fifth hole is a bit longer. At 453 yards form the back tees, this par 4 can prove to be a good test for the golfer. A mighty drive down the right center of the fairway is optimal. Mounding along the left creates interesting uphill, downhill and sidehill combinations.

A fairly long approach can be expected into the green. By using at least one more club than what is usually required, falling short of the green due to strong headwind can be avoided.

This green is the only one on the course without a bunker. If the ball is in the sand after the second shot, it must have been hit way off line! The approach should be hit directly for the hole; safety is assured on this green. The flat putting surface accommodates good putts.

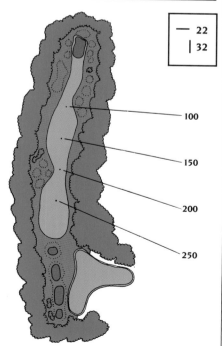

— 22
| 32

100

150

200

250

OYSTER REEF GOLF CLUB

6

	GOLD	BLUE	WHITE	RED
YDS:	192	160	146	122
PAR:	3	3	3	3
HDCP:	15	15	15	15

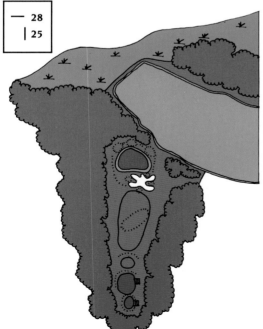

— 28

| 25

Oyster Reef's signature hole. The ocean has come into view. That means the winds will be picking up. Club selection is vital. A strong headwind will easily add 30 yards to the length.

One large bunker lies ominously to the right front. Play the tee shot long and to the left side of the green, thereby avoiding a tricky bunker shot. Be careful, however, to stay out of the trees along the left. The trees and even the out of bounds stakes will impede a good score.

The short wide green rolls gently in the middle. Putts longer than 20 feet will most likely have to navigate a slope or two. Green in one, two putts, and a par — on to the next hole!

OYSTER REEF GOLF CLUB

	GOLD	BLUE	WHITE	RED
YDS:	400	368	346	292
PAR:	4	4	4	4
HDCP:	11	11	11	13

7

The angle from the tee box on the left actually provides a better view to the fairway than from the tees on the right. These Gold tees, however, also add a few yards and a little bit of water that must be transited.

From either tees, the drive should be played directly down the middle of the fairway. Too far left and the trees will block the approach; too far right and the trees will block the approach! A medium-length approach should be planned for.

The bunkers surrounding the back side of the green necessitate an accurate second shot. Any stray off line will find the sand. The small flat putting surface has potential for yielding one putts.

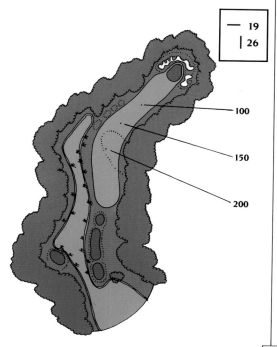

— 19
| 26

100

150

200

OYSTER REEF GOLF CLUB

8

	GOLD	BLUE	WHITE	RED
YDS:	430	400	382	326
PAR:	4	4	4	4
HDCP:	1	1	1	5

— 29
| 28

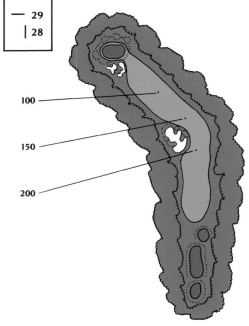

100

150

200

The eighth demands a strong, accurate drive. The large bunker at the corner of the dogleg catches many tee shots. Although the right does not look open, there is actually a lot of room for a drive.

Aim the tee shot just right of the bunker. Care should be taken to keep the ball in the fairway, since the trees and the sand can make the approach shot that much more difficult.

The putting surface is elevated and guarded by bunkers on the left front. Mounding around the backside helps to keep the longer approach within the putting area. Bogeys are abundant on this hole, be discouraged. The ninth is yet to be played, and birdies are always possible there!

OYSTER REEF GOLF CLUB

	GOLD	BLUE	WHITE	RED
YDS:	542	511	478	455
PAR:	5	5	5	5
HDCP:	7	7	7	3

9

The second shot is played down the left side of the fairway. The large bunkers along the right are best avoided. Also, keeping the ball left will assure a good angle at which the green is easily approached.

The green is small and flat. Bunkers surround the area, taking any mishit shots. Accuracy is a necessity. The birdie is always a great way to finish the front nine, although a par can be just as exciting on this hole!

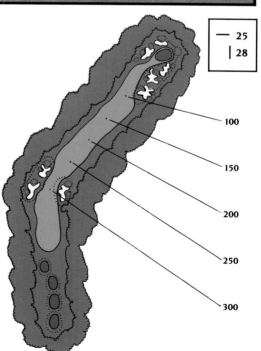

	GOLD	BLUE	WHITE	RED
10				
YDS:	387	353	343	320
PAR:	4	4	4	4
HDCP:	12	12	12	12

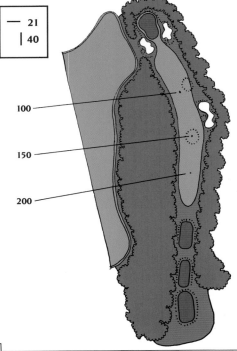

— 21
| 40

100

150

200

This medium-length par 4 is a good starting hole for the back side. The elevated tee area helps to uplift lagging spirits. A solid drive down the middle will set up a perfect approach.

The second shot is into a prevailing breeze, so club selection is important. Care must be taken to note the position of the pin. A long three-tiered green is the target.

OYSTER REEF GOLF CLUB

	GOLD	BLUE	WHITE	RED	**11**
YDS:	171	135	130	93	
PAR:	3	3	3	3	
HDCP:	18	18	18	16	

Water, water, water and more water! That's where a lot of golf balls end up on this hole. The tees are tucked in snuggly among the pines. The green is well backed by the trees. However, the front is all water. The shot off the tee is very important.

Take your time in deciding how to play the tee shot. Since the tee area and the green are protected, one may be unaware of the winds over the water. Careful planning will get the ball on the green.

The long green is deceiving from the tee. A large ridge runs across the putting surface, from left to right. Long tricky putts will test the authority of the putter.

—	18
	30

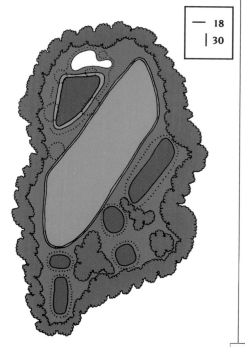

OYSTER REEF GOLF CLUB

12

	GOLD	BLUE	WHITE	RED
YDS:	524	491	470	414
PAR:	5	5	5	5
HDCP:	14	14	14	4

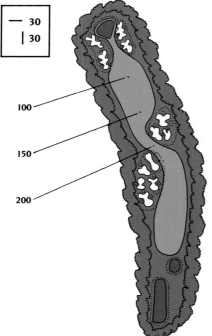

— 30
| 30

100

150

200

A grand total of twelve bunkers are present on this hole! The driving area is similar to a mine field. Although length is not a factor, ball control is a must.

Play the drive along the right side of the fairway. The fairway bunkers along the left side are merciless. If the sand is reached on the drive, you'll need superb for a good lie.

The second shot should be hit straight down the middle. A short approach can be expected to the large green.

The putting surface is flat at the rear and slopes slowly toward the front. The third shot should have been hit tight. Birdies are bountiful.

OYSTER REEF GOLF CLUB

	GOLD	BLUE	WHITE	RED
YDS:	423	385	363	328
PAR:	4	4	4	4
HDCP:	8	8	8	6

13

This thirteenth can be tough. A big drive off the tee must be long enough to get you within view of the green. Two large fairway bunkers sit on the corner. The bunkers are situated on top of mounding, which calls for a careful drive.

The tee shot should be played down the left side of the fairway. The following approach must be hit strongly to get up to the flag. The bunkers on either side of the green are deep and difficult.

The elevated putting surface is flat and large. The ball must be hit close in order for a one putt. A bogey here is acceptable.

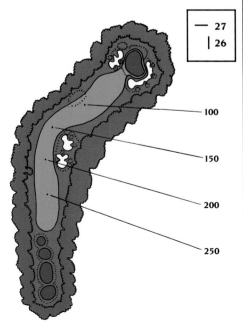

— 27
| 26

100

150

200

250

OYSTER REEF GOLF CLUB

14		GOLD	BLUE	WHITE	RED
	YDS:	384	362	340	266
	PAR:	4	4	4	4
	HDCP:	4	4	4	10

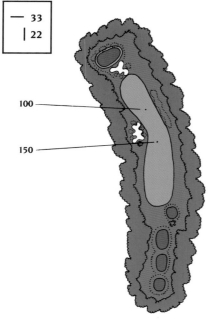

— 33
| 22

100

150

This hole is very tight. The drive must be hit with accuracy to the right side of the fairway. A ditch along the right will attract any shot that comes too close. The large bunker to the left is bordered by mounding, leaving little room for escape.

A drive to the outside corner of the dogleg is optimal. Care must be taken so that the shot does not bound through the fairway. A fairway wood or long iron may be the best choice from the tee.

The second shot must be delicately hit over the long bunker in front of the green. The short, wide green is easily mastered with the putter, but you have to be on the putting surface to use the putter. Knock the approach to the center of the green.

OYSTER REEF GOLF CLUB

	GOLD	BLUE	WHITE	RED	
YDS:	541	504	470	429	**15**
PAR:	5	5	5	5	
HDCP:	10	10	10	8	

This double dogleg is undoubtedly one of the better par 5's on the island. A long drive down the middle will set up for a second shot, again down the middle.
The third shot must stay clear of the bunkers and land close to the hole.

Usually into the wind, the tee shot is the most important shot on this hole. The trees along the left and the bunkers to the right must be avoided. The mounding along the right side gives the illusion of a very narrow fairway. But don't be fooled. Go for a simple drive down the middle.

The second shot should be played along the right middle of the fairway. An open approach, well away from the pond to the left, will allow for an easy lofted shot to the green.

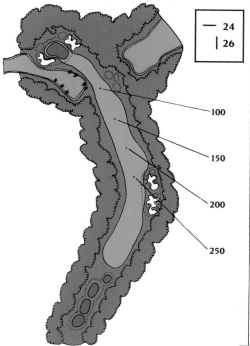

— 24
| 26

100

150

200

250

OYSTER REEF GOLF CLUB

16

	GOLD	BLUE	WHITE	RED
YDS:	209	165	145	107
PAR:	3	3	3	3
HDCP:	16	16	16	18

— 28
| 38

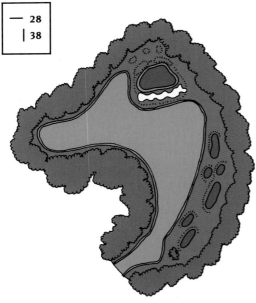

A solid well-hit tee shot is imperative. The six teeing areas allow for many different angles to the green. Care must be taken to note the actual distance from your tee shot to the green. The wide bunker in front of the green will help stop shots that have ended up short and start rolling backwards.

One more club than necessary is advised to assure a carry over the water. The large wide green has a slight roll in the center, but that is the least of the concerns. Once on the putting surface, take the two putts and proceed to the next hole. A par on this hole will be tough for the competition.

OYSTER REEF GOLF CLUB

	GOLD	BLUE	WHITE	RED
YDS:	453	412	388	344
PAR:	4	4	4	4
HDCP:	2	2	2	2

17

Into the wind, this seventeenth can be a long, demanding hole. A mighty drive down the left middle of the fairway is a requirement. A tee shot that slips a bit to the right may discover the water. A pull left could careen out of bounds.

The second shot will most likely be a long approach. Bunkers left and right necessitate a straight shot to the green. With the wind blowing and the green too far to reach in two, simply play the hole as a par 5 and birdie it!

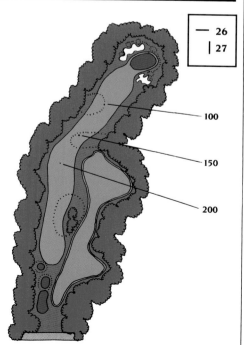

— 26
| 27

100

150

200

OYSTER REEF GOLF CLUB

18

	GOLD	BLUE	WHITE	RED
YDS:	461	421	407	337
PAR:	4	4	4	4
HDCP:	6	6	6	14

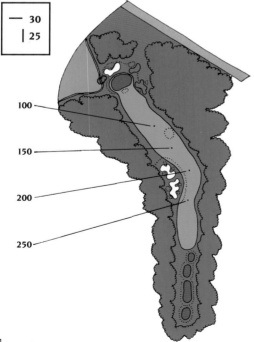

The eighteenth does not let up the pressure. If the match has come down to this hole, play it safe and keep the ball in the short grass. A smooth swing with the driver should guide the ball just right of the bunkers to the left. The second shot must be played directly for the center of the green. The bunkers to the right and beyond will probably not come into play if the ball is kept to the center of the green.

The flat putting surface appears very short from the fairway. Do not be tricked; simply hit the ball onto the green. A little bit of concentration will get the ball into the cup on the first try.

OYSTER REEF GOLF CLUB

Hilton Head Plantation
P.O. Box 22419
Hilton Head Island, SC 29925
803-681-7717
Semi-Private

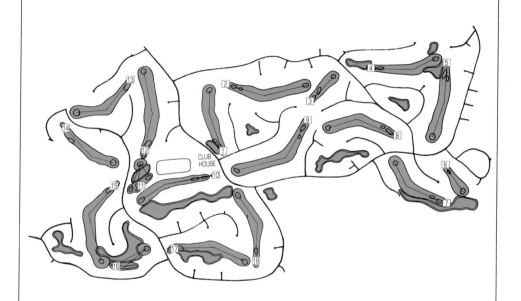

Course	Rating	Slope
Gold	73.7	131
Blue	71.2	123
White	69.5	118
Red	70.1	118

Head Professional: Mike Bartholomew
Superintendent: Donnie Smith
Designers: Rees Jones

HOLE	1	2	3	4	5	6	7	8	9	OUT	10	11	12	13	14	15	16	17	18	IN	TOTAL
GOLD	391	514	175	375	455	192	400	430	542	3474	387	171	524	423	384	541	209	453	461	3553	7027
BLUE	364	480	168	364	397	160	368	400	511	3212	353	135	491	385	362	504	165	412	421	3228	6440
WHITE	342	463	145	341	372	146	346	382	478	3015	343	130	470	363	340	470	145	388	407	3056	6071
HDCP	13	9	17	5	3	15	11	1	7		12	18	14	8	4	10	16	2	6		
PAR	4	5	3	4	4	3	4	4	5	36	4	3	5	4	4	5	3	4	4	36	72
RED	267	427	118	317	326	122	292	326	455	2650	320	93	414	328	266	429	107	344	337	2638	5288
HDCP	11	1	17	9	7	15	13	5	3		12	18	4	6	10	8	18	2	14		

LONG COVE CLUB

The Plantation

Long Cove Plantation is a private residential community encompassing 610 acres of golf, tennis, swimming and boating. Centrally located on Hilton Head Island, the plantation offers easy accessibility to the area.

The Course

As for the golf course itself, it was opened for play in 1981 and is considered one of the finest in the region. Pete Dye's unique style of design gives the Long Cove Club a Scottish flavor which intensifies the beauty of the course.

The front nine opens with a few holes that will keep the golfer on his toes. Water is the major ingredient. The fifth hole is one that will be talked about when the round is finished; mounding blocks the green from view. The next few holes are right out of the old country. Love grass accentuates the mounding on the sides of the rolling fairways. As the front nine comes to a close, one will discover that both accuracy and length are necessities on this course.

The back nine turns out toward the west, starting off with a par 4 that is almost a mirror image of the first hole. The creative use of mounding on the first few holes of the back side prove that a golf hole does not have to be long to be a good test of golfing ability. The thirteenth and fourteenth holes meander out toward the intercoastal. The marsh grass is picturesque, but it's also intimidating to the golfer. Dye wraps up the eighteen with a hole romantically reminiscent of the old Scottish courses. Long Cove is a magnificent golf course!

LONG COVE CLUB

	GOLD	BLUE	WHITE	RED
YDS:	400	390	358	334
PAR:	4	4	4	4
HDCP:	7	7	7	5

1

It becomes apparent very quickly that this golf course is not easily conquered. Pete Dye has put his best into this super layout. The first hole starts off with a slight dogleg right. Water down the right adds to the difficulty. A lone bunker along the left is the guide for the drive. Play the tee shot just right of the bunker and let the ball move right. A fairly long approach shot can be expected into the large rolling green. Since the water and bunker are right, keep the second shot to the left center of the putting surface. Roll the first putt close for the easy tap-in. Starting conservatively will be beneficial as the round continues.

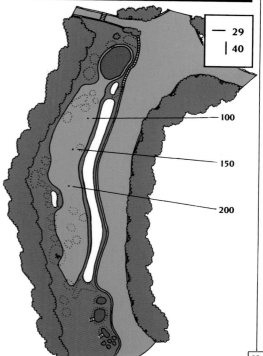

— 29

| 40

— 100

— 150

— 200

LONG COVE CLUB

2

	GOLD	BLUE	WHITE	RED
YDS:	196	151	145	94
PAR:	3	3	3	3
HDCP:	17	17	17	17

— 28
| 35

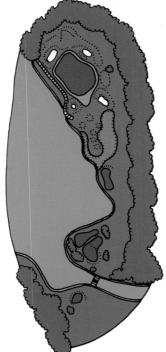

From the back tees, the green can be seen beyond a long stretch of water. The carry is not that bad unless the wind is blowing. Unfortunately, this can happen at the most inopportune time — when it's your turn! If the water is not intimidating, take a look at the bunkers surrounding the green. The *only* way to play this hole is to knock the tee shot to the center of the green. Two putts and on to the third.

LONG COVE CLUB

	GOLD	BLUE	WHITE	RED
YDS:	539	527	503	446
PAR:	5	5	5	5
HDCP:	1	1	1	1

3

Wow! Even if this hole was short, it still would be difficult! Water sneaks in from the right and winds its way up the left side of the hole. A solid drive must carry the water, stay right of the bunker and land somewhere just short of the bunker on the right. Favor the right side since the trees will give you a second chance for a shot, unlike the water, which will add a penalty stroke to the score.

A second shot should be played down the middle, leaving an approach shot of about 150 yards left to the green.

The putting surface is wedged in between mounding right and water left. The shape can be deceiving. Note the long swing the green takes to the left and be sure to use enough club! Pars are valuable but birdies will win the hole!

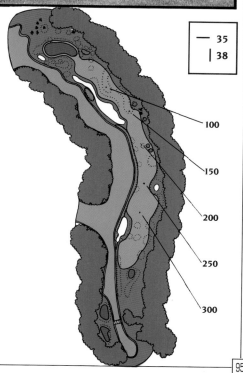

— 35
| 38

100

150

200

250

300

LONG COVE CLUB

	GOLD	BLUE	WHITE	RED
YDS:	384	359	344	294
PAR:	4	4	4	4
HDCP:	11	11	11	9

4

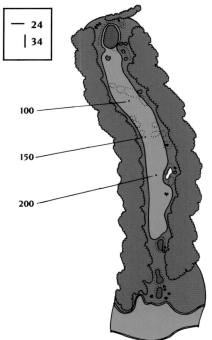

— 24
| 34

100
150
200

Finally, a hole which can produce an easy birdie or two. Length is not the main factor. What Pete Dye has done instead is to roll the fairway, adding another dimension to the hole. A sidehill — downhill lie may be found for the approach. Trees come in from both sides near the green for intimidation. Go long; bunkers short right will be out of play and the trees will easily be cleared. If too long, a simple chip down to the hole will take care of saving the par.

	GOLD	BLUE	WHITE	RED
	L O N G C O V E C L U B			
YDS:	317	290	276	239
PAR:	4	4	4	4
HDCP:	13	13	13	13

5

Take a good look at the green from the tee; it can not be seen from the fairway. The drive must be placed delicately beyond the fairway bunker to the right. A short approach to the green must be lofted softly over the large mounding in front of the green. Short, and the ball may grvitate to a bunker nestled in the side of the hill, or it may be kicked across the green. Too long and . . . into the water. The putting surface rolls downward from back to front.

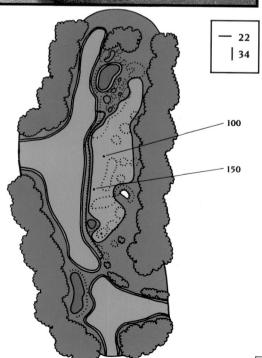

— 22
| 34

100

150

	GOLD	BLUE	WHITE	RED
YDS:	513	509	498	425
PAR:	5	5	5	5
HDCP:	5	5	5	3

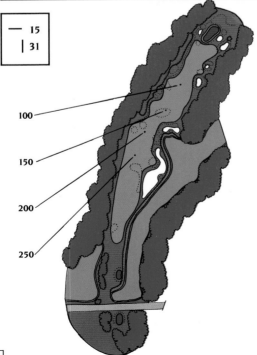

When teeing off the back tees it is advisable to check both left and right first. The drive must be carried over a road, left of the water and sand, and find its way to the center of the fairway. The water wraps around the fairway bunker, so care must be taken on the second shot to keep the ball down the left side. The fairway slopes left to right, and a shot along the left will be guided towards the center.

The approach is made to a green which is cut into the side of a hill. Any shots left have a chance of being coaxed to the putting surface. Shots to the right can necessitate a chip shot back to the green.

LONG COVE CLUB

	GOLD	BLUE	WHITE	RED
YDS:	439	430	388	308
PAR:	4	4	4	4
HDCP:	3	3	3	7

7

Length is back in the game. A firm drive up the left center of the fairway will position the ball perfectly for an approach to the green. The elevated putting surface is similar to the last hole in that it's cut into the side of a hill. A large bunker right will grab all those who stray too far in that direction. The surface is lowest on the middle left side. Tricky putts over the ridge will test the credentials of the putter.

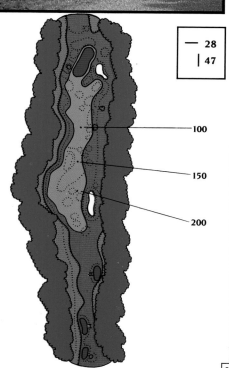

— 28
| 47

100

150

200

LONG COVE CLUB

8

	GOLD	BLUE	WHITE	RED
YDS:	203	195	155	117
PAR:	3	3	3	3
HDCP:	15	15	15	15

— 21
| 40

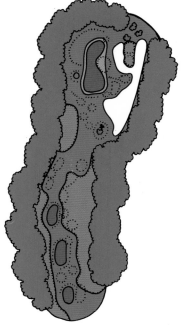

So picturesque, yet so menacing. This is not the time to raise the bet. Love grass grows abundantly throughout the green. The elevated tee gives a downward view on the putting surface. Keep your attention focused there. A strong tee shot (using enough club) is required to get the ball to the cup. The large area of sand to the right is more than enough to make a par save nearly impossible.

LONG COVE CLUB

	GOLD	BLUE	WHITE	RED
YDS:	428	375	329	272
PAR:	4	4	4	4
HDCP:	9	9	9	11

9

Players on the back tees must give way to automobile traffic again. This ninth hole finishes the front without mercy. The best drive is played right along the edge of the fairway, leaving an approach of less than 150 yards. Trees left and right reach in to intimidate. A large bunker starts 90 yards out and continues up to the green. Keep the approach long and left center. The water is back in play here! If all goes well the crowd up at the clubhouse will murmur admiringly when the birdie putt is knocked to the center of the cup!

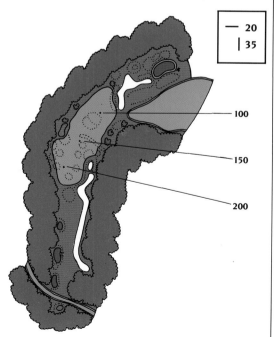

— 20
| 35

100

150

200

LONG COVE CLUB

	GOLD	BLUE	WHITE	RED
YDS:	403	387	346	296
PAR:	4	4	4	4
HDCP:	10	10	10	14

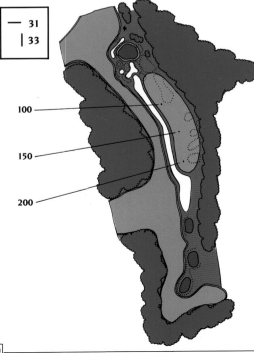

— 31
| 33

100

150

200

The tenth hole is a mirror image of the first. The drive should be played down the middle of the fairway. The water and sand left, along with the solid row of trees right, narrow the target area. Swirling winds can cause a seemingly perfect approach shot to stray off line. A grass bunker lies short right and sand bunkers are left. Once on the putting surface, the putts should roll true.

LONG COVE CLUB

	GOLD	BLUE	WHITE	RED
YDS:	376	368	326	311
PAR:	4	4	4	4
HDCP:	14	14	14	10

Dye has sculptured this eleventh into a hole that proves that length is not necessary to have a good golf hole. By aiming the drive down the left side, you will set the ball into perfect position for the approach. Violent rolling of the fairway fills the view between the drive and the green. An accurate shot to the center of the green is required in order to keep the pars coming.

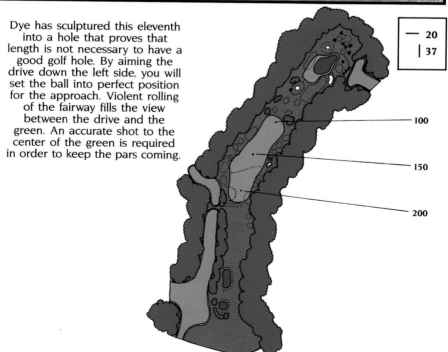

— 20
| 37

100

150

200

LONG COVE CLUB

12

	GOLD	BLUE	WHITE	RED
YDS:	445	397	379	313
PAR:	4	4	4	4
HDCP:	4	4	4	4

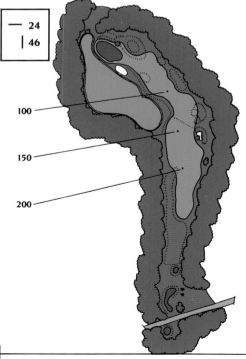

— 24
| 46

100

150

200

The Gold tees play this twelfth hole from back across the road. (Be sure to check both ways before crossing!) The drive should be played up the left center of the fairway. Note the water hazard that squeezes into the picture. From the fairway bunker on the right to the water on the left, the fairway slopes down toward the hole. A plateau is formed. Hopefully the tee shot will come to rest either short of the edge or through the slope into the flat ground. A downhill lie can cause havoc with the approach shot.

The putting surface slopes slowly toward the front. Accuracy wil be helpful in order to keep the ball on target. Play the second shot to the right for safety. A short chip shot can be hit close to save par, if needed.

LONG COVE CLUB

	GOLD	BLUE	WHITE	RED
YDS:	137	130	116	84
PAR:	3	3	3	3
HDCP:	18	18	18	18

13

Broad Creek waterway is in sight. Do not let the transient boats intimidate you on this shot to the green. Target golf is the game here. Swirling wind can cause a bit of uncertainty at the tee. Play the ball strong — never up, never in. Pin placement is the least of the concerns. Getting the ball on the putting surface is important to get by this hole successfully. Once on the green, the putt should roll nicely.

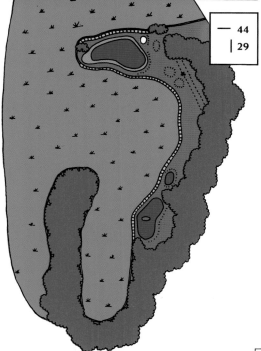

— 44
| 29

LONG COVE CLUB

14

	GOLD	BLUE	WHITE	RED
YDS:	410	374	352	291
PAR:	4	4	4	4
HDCP:	6	6	6	6

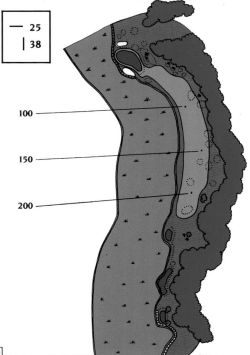

— 25

| 38

100

150

200

If the ball can be hit 380 yards on the fly, go for the green! Nothing but marsh lies between the tee and the green. The green can be seen easily. However, Pete Dye has designed the hole so that it must be played to the right and then to the green.

A solid tee shot to the right center of the fairway will set up a good angle for the approach. Be careful that the wind is not blowing right to left, and take a good tee shot into the marsh.

The approach is delicate. Keep the ball to the right as long as possible, then bring it left onto the putting surface. Two putts and a par. Simple!

LONG COVE CLUB				
	GOLD	BLUE	WHITE	RED
YDS:	590	557	495	439
PAR:	5	5	5	5
HDCP:	2	2	2	2

15

The fifteenth stretches out a bit — nearly 600 yards from the gold tees! Three well-hit shots are required to get home in regulation. A strong drive down the right center is a must to start out with. The second shot should be played just left of center. One bunker on the right side and a few bunkers along the left can make the third shot that much more difficult.

Trees situated on either side of the green stand guard around the hole. Slip the approach through the middle and watch the ball come to rest inches from the cup. A birdie on this hole justifies bragging rights back at the clubhouse.

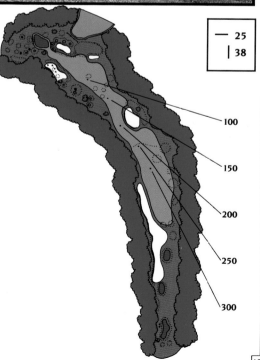

— 25
| 38

100

150

200

250

300

	GOLD	BLUE	WHITE	RED
YDS:	460	389	354	311
PAR:	4	4	4	4
HDCP:	12	12	12	12

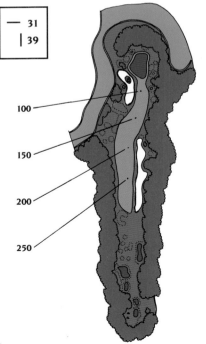

— 31
| 39

100

150

200

250

Hopefully the last hole got your long game in shape. It will be needed on this hole! A good solid drive down the left center of the fairway will put the ball into ideal position for the approach.

A long approach can be expected. A large bunker and trees on the left side attract many shots. Play safe and keep the ball right.

LONG COVE CLUB

	GOLD	BLUE	WHITE	RED	
YDS:	210	172	143	116	**17**
PAR:	3	3	3	3	
HDCP:	16	16	16	16	

One of Dye's trademarks is the short par 3 with abundant water. This allows a good par 3 to provide a challenge without being excessively long. Well, that holds true for most of his par 3's! This hole, from the Gold tees, can play longer than the 210 yards if the wind is blowing.

A thick line of trees on the left does not allow a safe shot to the left. Consequently, play the tee shot straight for the center of the green. Pars will keep the game alive.

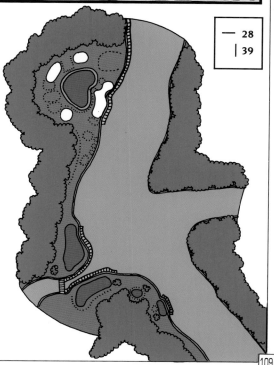

— 28
| 39

L O N G   C O V E   C L U B

18		GOLD	BLUE	WHITE	RED
	YDS:	450	420	366	312
	PAR:	4	4	4	4
	HDCP:	8	8	8	8

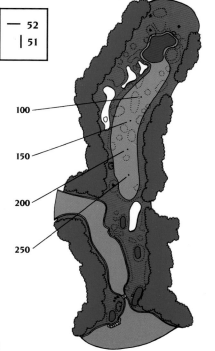

— 52

| 51

100

150

200

250

The eighteenth finishes with style. The fairway rolls violently right and left. Bunkers along the left will hinder those who get a little too strong on the last drive. The old country comes to mind as you stroll up to the mounded green.

A solid drive down the center of the fairway gets the hole started well. A long approach into the elevated green will most likely be the results. Swing smoothly and knock the second shot up to the heart of the putting surface. Give the onlookers at the clubhouse a thrill. The large undalating green will leave some very long tricky putts. Remember to get the first putt close to the hole so that the second can be tapped in easily.

LONG COVE CLUB

Long Cove Plantation
Hilton Head Island, SC 29926
803-842-5558
Private

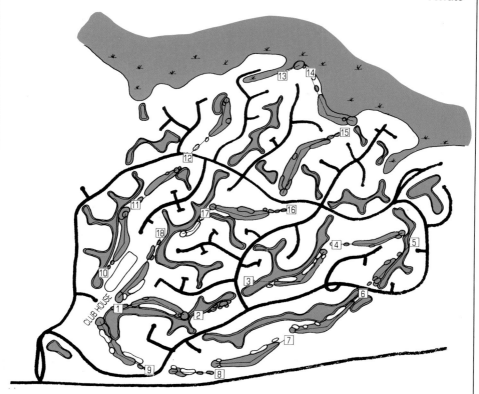

Course	Rating	Slope
Gold	74.3	140
Blue	71.9	128
White	69.9	123
Red	69.5	114

Head Professional: Bob Patton
Designer: Pete Dye

HOLE	1	2	3	4	5	6	7	8	9	OUT	10	11	12	13	14	15	16	17	18	IN	TOTAL
GOLD	400	196	539	384	317	513	439	203	428	3419	403	376	445	137	410	590	460	210	450	3481	6900
BLUE	390	151	527	359	290	509	430	195	375	3226	387	368	397	130	374	557	389	172	420	3194	6420
WHITE	358	145	503	344	276	498	388	155	329	2996	346	326	379	116	352	495	354	143	366	2877	5873
HDCP	7	17	1	11	13	5	3	15	9		10	14	4	18	6	2	12	16	8		
PAR	4	3	5	4	4	5	4	3	4	36	4	4	4	3	4	5	4	3	4	35	72
RED	334	94	446	294	239	425	308	117	272	2529	296	311	313	84	291	439	311	116	312	2437	5002
HDCP	5	17	1	9	13	3	7	15	11		14	10	4	18	6	2	12	16	8		

The Plantation

Located at the geographical center of Hilton Head Island, Palmetto Dunes enjoys three miles of Atlantic Ocean beaches within its 2,000 acres. An eleven-mile manmade lagoon system, winds throughout, providing the many water hazards for the golf courses. Three championship layouts meander through the rolling landscape of the plantation. The courses include:

Arthur Hills Course

George Fazio Course

Robert Trent Jones Course

ARTHUR HILLS
GOLF COURSE

The Course

Arthur Hills Golf Course is one of the youngest courses on Hilton Head Island. Opened for play in Spring 1986, the Hills course has drawn attention for its unique characteristics. The perfect blend of Scottish heritage and the natural rolls of the land amplify the beauty in the golf course. Unfortunately, beauty has its price. This Hills course is a challenge!

The front nine begins with a few short par 4's. Simple enough — except for the fact that the fairways roll unpredictably, providing for some interesting sidehill lies. The first green is hidden by mounding and the second is placed delicately on the edge of a pond. Hopefully, your game is up to par, since the course only gets tougher as you go along. The last few holes, on the front side, demand the best from the long hitter. Severe pitching of the fairway requires planning of each shot in order to take advantage of the roll and deflection from the small hills.

The tenth hole, with its length and narrowness, establishes the authority of the course. The eleventh hole features an elevated tee that overlooks the long narrow green — a par 3, which would normally be found in more hilly regions. The twelfth hole introduces the menacing waterways. This is where the course can become tricky. The narrow fairway requires a delicately placed drive to avoid the trees and also the water. A bit of creativity would not hurt here. The course finishes with two very difficult holes. The par 4, seventeenth, requires well-placed shots. The eighteenth leads off with a blind drive and plays to a green hidden by mounding. The course keeps you fighting to the end.

ARTHUR HILLS GOLF COURSE

	BLUE	WHITE	RED
YDS:	384	358	284
PAR:	4	4	4
HDCP:	13	13	15

1

Arthur Hills has yet to reveal his secrets on this hole. Straight-away, the hole is simple enough. However, the rolling fairway will add a third dimension. A large pine is found down the left side. It is best to keep the drive right to avoid the tree and get a clear shot to the green. Hidden amongst the mounds, the putting surface is a fairly large target to aim for. Bunker back right corner will grab any long approaches.

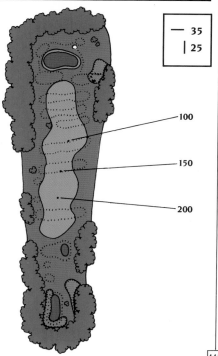

— 35
| 25

100

150

200

2

	BLUE	WHITE	RED
YDS:	373	334	289
PAR:	4	4	4
HDCP:	3	3	1

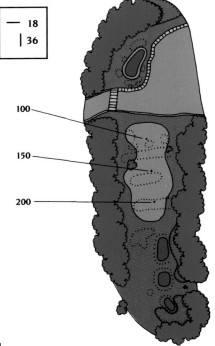

The large oak on the left side of the fairway will prevent any open shots from that direction. It is important to keep the drive to the right, but not too long. Back off the driver a bit and play for position. It is worth the effort to be on the right side for the approach. The carry is over the water to a green that has a slight roll crossing the middle. Keep dry and snug; there's more water to deal with at the next hole.

The main concern here is to avoid the water. However, do not over-correct and end up out of bounds to the left. A solid shot to the center of the green is the best strategy. Make a point to use one more club than necessary to not only carry the water hazard, but to also get past the bunker in front.

— 31
| 33

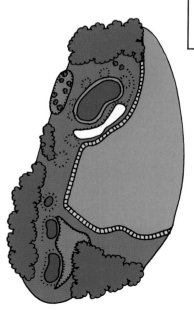

ARTHUR HILLS GOLF COURSE

4

	BLUE	WHITE	RED
YDS:	430	403	294
PAR:	4	4	4
HDCP:	11	11	9

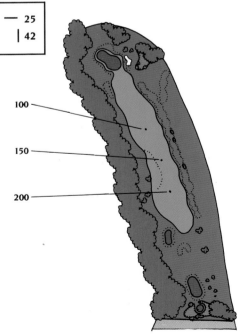

— 25
| 42

100

150

200

The large mounding to the right on this hole creates the sensation of being in a valley. The hole bends around to the left, with a solid wall of trees at the corner. Playing the drive up the right side of the fairway will yield several advantages. The slope of the mounding will direct the ball back to the center. Result: a few extra yards on the stroke. Play it strong, but be careful not to go over the mound. You'll be stuck with a blind shot to the hole.

The elevated tee box is out of character for these lowlands. Not a very long hole, this par five is still a test of skill. Keep the ball off to the right. The trees to the left can and will block any approach shots that were left short off the tee. A large bunker to the front is the only bunker on the fifth, but it's a big one. Get the ball close to the flag. This large green may require a few extra putts.

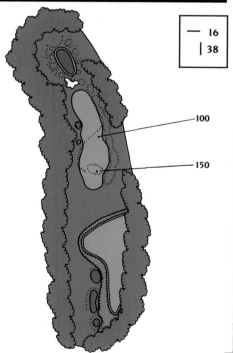

— 16
| 38

100

150

ARTHUR HILLS GOLF COURSE

6

	BLUE	WHITE	RED
YDS:	505	480	410
PAR:	5	5	5
HDCP:	9	9	11

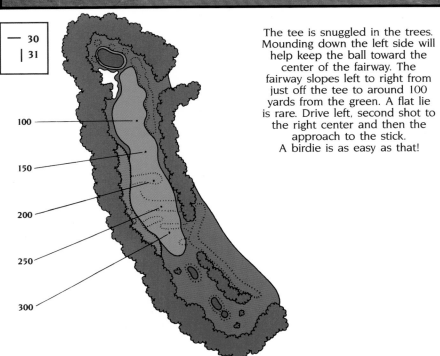

The tee is snuggled in the trees. Mounding down the left side will help keep the ball toward the center of the fairway. The fairway slopes left to right from just off the tee to around 100 yards from the green. A flat lie is rare. Drive left, second shot to the right center and then the approach to the stick. A birdie is as easy as that!

ARTHUR HILLS GOLF COURSE

	BLUE	WHITE	RED
YDS:	434	417	322
PAR:	4	4	4
HDCP:	1	1	7

7

Similar to the fourth, with the mounding down the right side, this seventh hole is just slightly longer, with a dogleg to the right. Obviously, the ball should be played down the left side, leaving an approach clear to the green. Usually into the wind, this hole presents a long approach to the green. Take it in stride. A five on this hole is something to be proud of.

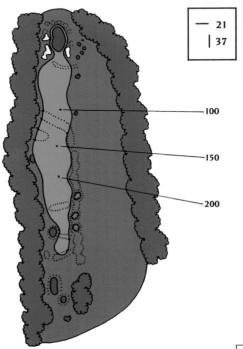

— 21

| 37

—— 100

—— 150

—— 200

ARTHUR HILLS GOLF COURSE

8

	BLUE	WHITE	RED
YDS:	156	135	113
PAR:	3	3	3
HDCP:	15	15	13

— 38
| 26

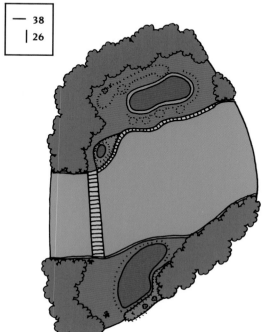

A fairly short par 3, this eighth should not be underestimated. Water dominates this hole, which is usually into the wind, so it;s important to use the right club. Expect the wind to be stronger above the tree line. Note the shortness of the green compared to its width. The tall pines beyond the green amplify this image of a short green. Threes are good on any par 3.

ARTHUR HILLS GOLF COURSE

	BLUE	WHITE	RED
YDS:	518	494	434
PAR:	5	5	5
HDCP:	7	7	5

9

The expanse of the fairway is obscured by the large mound that crosses in front of the tees. Back in line with the first hole, this ninth is hilly and tough. Keep the ball down the right side — all the way to the green. You may want to play the second shot to avoid the water hazard to the front and left of the green. Getting home in two is risky. Play conservatively. Lay up the second shot in position for an optimal third shot. Now is not the time to take chances.

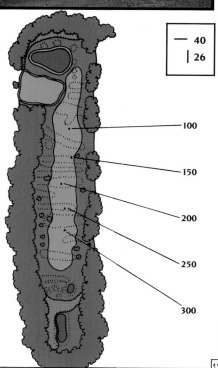

— 40
| 26

100

150

200

250

300

	BLUE	WHITE	RED
YDS:	415	392	312
PAR:	4	4	4
HDCP:	14	14	14

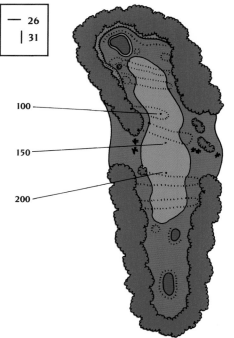

— 26
| 31

100

150

200

A wide open fairway — at last! There are no bunkers to contend with on this tenth hole. There is, however, a dogleg to go around. Play the drive down the right side in order to get a good view of the green for the approach. The mounding around the green creates a backboard type of effect.

A spectacular view from this eleventh tee. Well...almost. Besides the large area of love grass to transit and the green setting below tee level, amongst the trees and large bunkers, this hole is simple! Simply play the ball long enough to carry the love grass and avoid the bunkers. Once you're on the green, knock the putt in and go on to the next hole. (This is a pretty hole.)

— 23
| 33

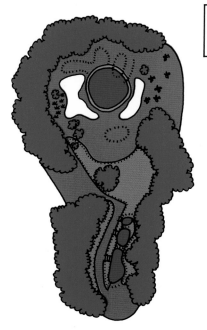

	BLUE	WHITE	RED
YDS:	399	377	296
PAR:	4	4	4
HDCP:	2	2	2

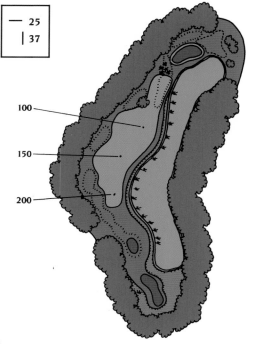

— 25

| 37

100

150

200

Wow! Lots of water! The green is easy to see to the right, but the ball must be played to the left first. Mounding down the left side will actually help to keep a few balls from going through the fairway. Try to get the ball to the center of the fairway. Trees left and water right make those sides unattractive. A long narrow green is the target. Notice how Hills is making these later holes a little bit more difficult.

ARTHUR HILLS GOLF COURSE

	BLUE	WHITE	RED
YDS:	507	486	338
PAR:	5	5	5
HDCP:	6	6	8

13

There is no mercy. This thirteenth is as difficult as it looks. In theory, the hole should be played with a drive down the middle, but don't be fooled. Chances of getting to the green in two are slim. A second shot should be played short and left of the water. The approach is then to one of the smallest greens on the course.
Par is a happy dividend.

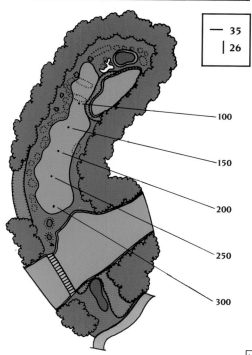

— 35
| 26

—100

—150

—200

—250

—300

ARTHUR HILLS GOLF COURSE

14

	BLUE	WHITE	RED
YDS:	412	361	301
PAR:	4	4	4
HDCP:	10	10	10

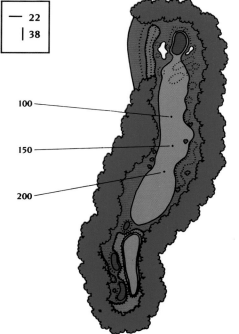

— 22
| 38

100
150
200

The tension is relieved, but not by much. The fourteenth is a solid par 4. Drive down the right side to get a peek around the corner. The green is long and two-tiered. Bunkers left and right will grab any stray shots.

As this lighthouse was used as a guide into safe harbour, it can be used to help guide the ball to this fifteenth green. The shot is made from an elevated tee to an elevated green. The oak trees around the green can be greedy, so play for the center. Single bunker front left is best avoided.

— 18
| 32

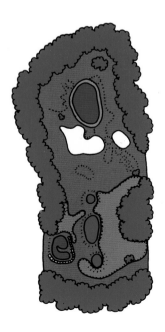

ARTHUR HILLS GOLF COURSE

16

	BLUE	WHITE	RED
YDS:	365	336	295
PAR:	4	4	4
HDCP:	8	8	12

— 27
| 48

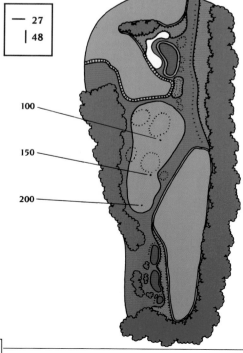

100

150

200

The tee seems to be out of a chute. Although the water to the right may influence the desire to play left, keep the ball right to avoid a large carry over the lagoon up nearer the green. This approach is to a long, long narrow green. Club selection is vital to a good score!

ARTHUR HILLS GOLF COURSE

	BLUE	WHITE	RED
YDS:	380	320	274
PAR:	4	4	4
HDCP:	4	4	4

17

So far, the water hazards have been on the right. But now it's on the left. That may be good — or it could be bad. The fairway is barely visible from the tee, but out there it is! The fairway actually opens up, so a drive down the right center is advised. The approach is delicate. You'll probably be playing into the wind, so it's important to use enough club to get to the green. Note the shape of the green. A pin placement in the back right corner will be tricky to get to. Birdie three justifies bragging rights in the clubhouse.

— 34
| 27

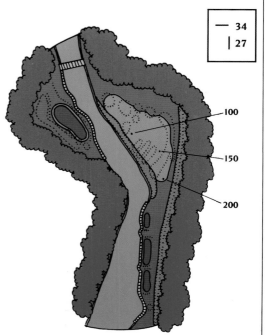

100

150

200

	BLUE	WHITE	RED
YDS:	516	497	414
PAR:	5	5	5
HDCP:	12	12	6

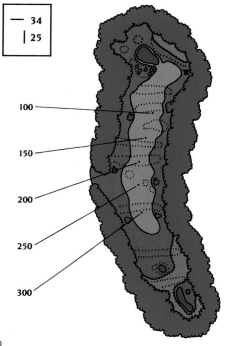

— 34
| 25

100
150
200
250
300

The final hole, the eighteenth, is the longest on the course. Not only that, the tee shot is blind and the green is hidden. Arthur Hills has saved his most fiendish tricks for last! Play the drive down the left center. In order to get a glimpse of the flag, you should play the second shot down the right side. Rolling fairway keeps the third dimension in the game. A large mound short and right of the green blocks the view of the green. Bunkers speckle the front of the mound. However they are of no concern if the approach is hit accurately. The putting surface is surrounded by mounds, giving it a bowl characteristic.

ARTHUR HILLS GOLF COURSE

Palmetto Dunes Plantation
P.O. Box 5849
Hilton Head Island, SC 29938
803-785-1138
Resort

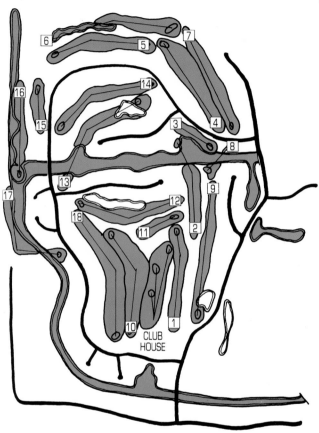

Course	Rating	Slope
Blue	71.6	126
White	69.2	120
Red	67.7	113

Director of Golf: Chip Pellerin
Head Professional: Bob Faulkner
Superintendent: Tom Arneman
Designer: Arthur Hills

HOLE	1	2	3	4	5	6	7	8	9	OUT	10	11	12	13	14	15	16	17	18	IN	TOTAL
BLUE	384	373	146	430	376	505	434	156	518	3322	415	182	399	507	412	153	365	380	516	3329	6651
WHITE	358	334	115	403	343	480	417	135	494	3079	392	132	377	486	361	142	336	320	497	3043	6122
HDCP	13	3	17	11	5	9	1	15	7		14	16	2	6	10	18	8	4	12		
PAR	4	4	3	4	4	5	4	3	5	36	4	3	4	5	4	3	4	4	5	36	72
RED	284	289	88	294	301	410	322	113	434	2535	312	114	296	338	301	120	295	274	414	2464	4999
HDCP	15	1	17	9	3	11	7	13	5		14	16	2	8	10	18	12	4	6		

The Course

Designed by George Fazio and opened for play in 1974, this course has appeared on *Golf Digest's* list of the 100 best courses in America. The unique factor of having only two par 5's sets the Fazio course apart from the rest. But little does this affect the total yardage of the layout. At over 6800 yards, it is apparent that the par 4's are also long. The fairways are open and roll gently on the front nine. The back nine becomes more severe and tighter, demanding good position off the tee.

A slight dogleg par 4 starts off the front nine at a tough 432 yards. The second follows along at 562 yards. This means your long game must be in top form. An exceptional standout is the eighth, a par 4 at 431 yards. The drive is uphill, restricting view of the fairway and landing area. The large swell then falls steeply toward the elevated green; finding an awkward lie is very likely. The small green appears even smaller when faced with a 200-yard approach off the side of a hill! The ninth finishes the front with customary fashion — long dogleg par 4 requiring a very accurate approach to a green cut out of the side of a hill.

The back nine opens with opportunity. A par 5 at a mere 513 yards, the tenth hole actually can play a bit shorter. A solid drive down the middle may be kicked forward toward the green upon passing a ridge running across the fairway. Getting home in two is possible. Birdies are a given. Mr. Fazio increases his demands as the nine continues, finishing up with a dramatic seventeenth par 3, which requires a carry of 200 yards over the water. The eighteenth completes the day with a par 4 of 462 yards. Fazio is not exactly a walk in the park.

GEORGE FAZIO GOLF CLUB

1

	GOLD	BLUE	WHITE	RED
YDS:	432	393	385	355
PAR:	4	4	4	4
HDCP:	3	3	3	3

A tough starting hole. Although the fairway seems wide from the tee, it's important to keep the drive down the right center of the fairway. Slight rolling of the fairway is revealing of what is to come. A long narrow green is the target. Be sure the right club is used on the approach. These lengthy greens may be the cause of a few shots that go left, well away from the hole. A par is a good score to start out with, and it will get the adrenaline flowing for the rest of the course.

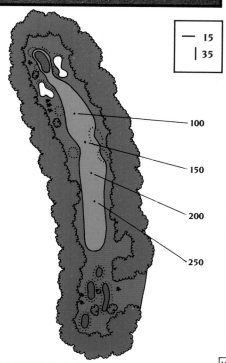

— 15
| 35

100

150

200

250

	GOLD	BLUE	WHITE	RED
YDS:	562	522	487	412
PAR:	5	5	5	5
HDCP:	11	11	11	1

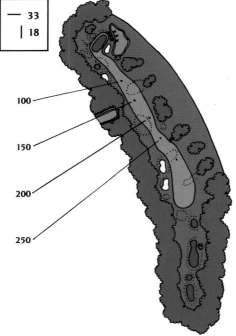

— 33

| 18

100

150

200

250

One of only two par 5's on this course, this second hole is the more difficult of the two. The view from the tee may give this fact away. Bunkers left and a narrow rolling fairway will instill a feeling of uncertainty upon address but, by playing the drive down the right center, the fairway bunkers will be avoided, and the ball will be in the best position for the second shot. Careful planning will help you keep clear of the water hazard near the green. A short approach to a wide, shallow green will have to be accurate for any chance of a birdie.

GEORGE FAZIO GOLF CLUB

	GOLD	BLUE	WHITE	RED
YDS:	412	412	396	357
PAR:	4	4	4	4
HDCP:	9	9	9	11

3

This old tree is a beautiful irony of nature — although old and gray, it is a wonderful sight. It is best viewed from the second shot which should be on the left side of the fairway. Greenside bunkers are deep, and also best viewed looking from afar. The putting surface slopes up and away from the fairway.
Make sure the correct club is used on the approach.

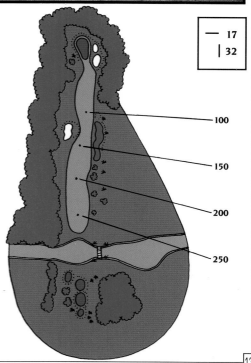

GEORGE FAZIO GOLF CLUB

4

	GOLD	BLUE	WHITE	RED
YDS:	205	195	190	137
PAR:	3	3	3	3
HDCP:	15	15	15	15

— 25
| 26

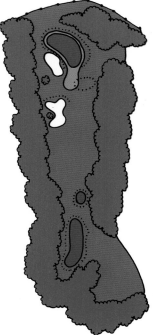

The first large bunker on the left is more intimidating than it should be. It's the second bunker on the left that can cause problems. The putting surface wraps around from the right. A pin placed just beyond the bunker adds to the difficulty. Play the shot off the tee to the right side of the green, moving it left as needed. A shot kept short and right is played more easily than the shot kept short on the left. Pars are worthy; bogeys are not to be disparaged.

GEORGE FAZIO GOLF CLUB

	GOLD	BLUE	WHITE	RED
YDS:	389	372	364	295
PAR:	4	4	4	4
HDCP:	7	7	7	13

5

Wow! This hole bends a bit! From the tee, the large fairway bunker is all that can be seen. Aim for it! (Just don't go into it!) Actually, playing the drive just left of the bunker is important in order to get around the trees on the left. A clear shot to the green is a necessity to get home in regulation.

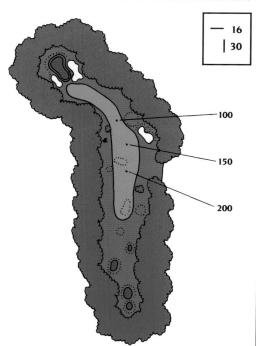

— 16
| 30

100

150

200

GEORGE FAZIO GOLF CLUB

6

	GOLD	BLUE	WHITE	RED
YDS:	180	167	156	136
PAR:	3	3	3	3
HDCP:	17	17	17	17

— 24
| 26

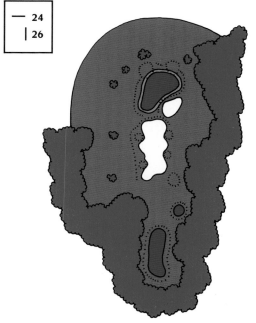

Not much between the tee and the green, except for maybe one large waste bunker. Shorter than the preceding par 3, this hole is just as demanding. The large bunker can be intimidating, although the bunker just right and short of the green will get most of the business. Play for the left side of the green, bringing it right as necessary.

GEORGE FAZIO GOLF CLUB

	GOLD	BLUE	WHITE	RED
YDS:	414	374	359	320
PAR:	4	4	4	4
HDCP:	5	5	5	9

7

The lagoon that crossed the path on the fourth hole has found its way back to cross in front of the green on this hole. A big drive, with the wind from behind, may find its way into the hazard off the tee. A mere 288 yards from the Gold tees, this water hazard is obviously best avoided. Back off on the driver and play for position. From either side of the fairway, the green is open for the approach. However, the putting surface is cut into the tree line like a corner pocket on a billiard table. Two bunkers front the forward sloping green.

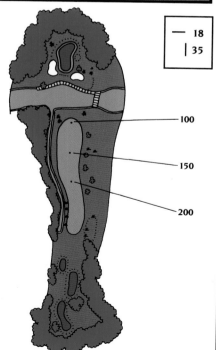

— 18
| 35

100

150

200

GEORGE FAZIO GOLF CLUB

8

	GOLD	BLUE	WHITE	RED
YDS:	431	422	421	342
PAR:	4	4	4	4
HDCP:	1	1	1	3

— 17
| 32

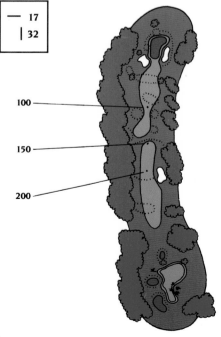

100

150

200

Over the hill it goes. Large bunker right implies that the better place to be is on the left. This is a long par four that requires a well-hit drive off the tee. From the drive, the second shot is played from the elevated fairway to an elevated green. Bunkers short, but sloping far, make the putting surface the best target. Par, even bogey, is acceptable.

GEORGE FAZIO GOLF CLUB

	GOLD	BLUE	WHITE	RED
YDS:	421	409	385	321
PAR:	4	4	4	4
HDCP:	13	13	13	7

9

Bunkers left and right, drive the ball down the center. The ninth is another long hole. Fazio is not giving you any breaks. The long, narrow green is overshadowed by the large bunker to the left. Unless you judge the distance on the approach accurately, you're going to discover you have a very lengthy putt.

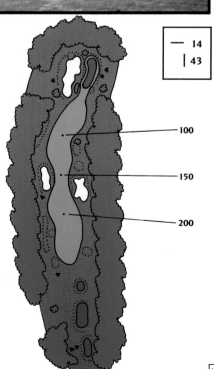

— 14
| 43

100

150

200

GEORGE FAZIO GOLF CLUB

10

	GOLD	BLUE	WHITE	RED
YDS:	513	513	485	438
PAR:	5	5	5	5
HDCP:	18	18	18	2

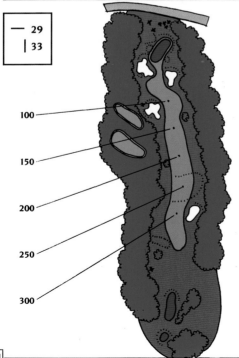

```
— 29
| 33
```

100

150

200

250

300

This is the second and last of the two par fives on the course. Handicapped as the easiest of all the holes, this par 5 is definitely an easy par, if not birdie, hole. From the tee it is difficult to see the green because of the large roll in the fairway. A well-hit drive down the middle will reward you with a fairly reachable distance to the green. Large bunkers — two left, one right — are best left alone. Play for the green on the second shot. A birdie will be an asset as the rest of the course is played out.

GEORGE FAZIO GOLF CLUB

	GOLD	BLUE	WHITE	RED
YDS:	394	376	364	320
PAR:	4	4	4	4
HDCP:	10	10	10	10

11

The green off in the distance is actually a double green that is also used for the fifteenth hole. The guy in the water is the guy who will make a hefty profit off all those shots not long enough to make the trip. Try not to contribute to the cause. Play the drive just left of the fairway bunker on the right. Bunkers are plentiful near the green, but as long as you get to the green in two, the bunkers should be of no concern.

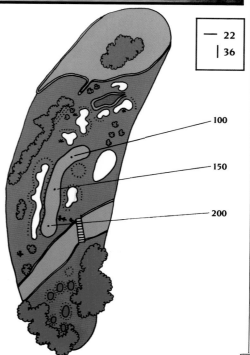

— 22
| 36

100

150

200

GEORGE FAZIO GOLF CLUB

12

	GOLD	BLUE	WHITE	RED
YDS:	387	364	319	275
PAR:	4	4	4	4
HDCP:	14	14	14	12

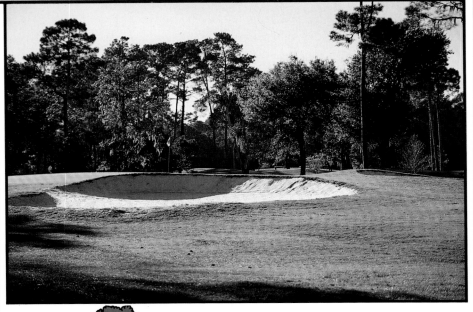

— 23

| 21

100

150

200

Water right should not present a problem. This twelfth hole is a short but challenging par 4. A well- placed drive down the middle is advised for a good position to get the second shot up on the putting surface. Two large bunkers lie ominously in the foreground. Maybe you should use one more club than neccessary to be sure of clearing these bunkers.

GEORGE FAZIO GOLF CLUB

	GOLD	BLUE	WHITE	RED
YDS:	386	366	354	279
PAR:	4	4	4	4
HDCP:	8	8	8	14

13

Very similar to number 5, this dogleg par 4 can cause some difficulty. By keeping the tee shot to the right, you will avoid the bunker on the left and stop with a clear opening to the green. Large bunker front right is best side-stepped to the left. Elevated green will test your putting skills.

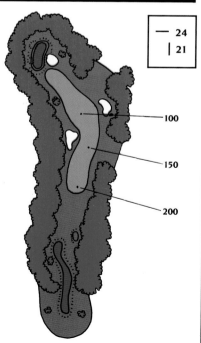

— 24
| 21

100

150

200

GEORGE FAZIO GOLF CLUB

14

	GOLD	BLUE	WHITE	RED
YDS:	185	164	150	123
PAR:	3	3	3	3
HDCP:	16	16	16	18

— 29
| 24

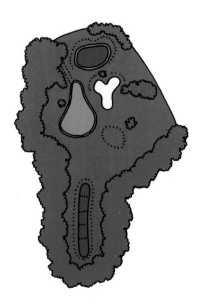

The water glistens with a thirst for golf balls, but a draw off the tee will keep the ball over the dry land. A bunker is easier to hit out of than water! However, up on the putting surface is the best place to take the second shot. A 3 on any par 3 is a good score, especially on this hole!

GEORGE FAZIO GOLF CLUB

	GOLD	BLUE	WHITE	RED
YDS:	445	414	410	342
PAR:	4	4	4	4
HDCP:	6	6	6	6

15

Water and sand hazards make the right side more appealing than the left. The perfect drive will be played down the right side of the fairway drawing slightly back to the left. Bounding over the mound, the ball would come to rest around the 150-yard marker. A crisp iron to the hole is best, bouncing by the cup, then spinning its way back to nestle up to the hole. Although it's a "gimme" the ball is stroked solidly to the bottom of the cup. Birdie. Next hole.

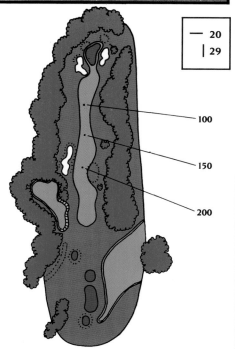

— 20
| 29

100

150

200

GEORGE FAZIO GOLF CLUB

16

	GOLD	BLUE	WHITE	RED
YDS:	425	416	403	349
PAR:	4	4	4	4
HDCP:	4	4	4	8

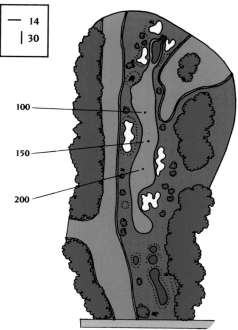

— 14
| 30

100

150

200

Large bunker just off the tee and slightly to the right gives a clue as to which side of the fairway the drive should be played. From the left side of the fairway, the second shot is played down the middle. The water that was seen on the left from the tee-box stays to the left all the way up the hole. However, another body of water presents itself up to the right. The edge of the hazard begins just 120 yards from the green and continues to alongside to the right. The approach is made to the putting surface hopefully avoiding the bunker left and the water right.

It is important to walk off this green in a positive frame of mind. The round is not over yet. Fazio still has a few tricks up his sleeve.

GEORGE FAZIO GOLF CLUB

	GOLD	BLUE	WHITE	RED
YDS:	230	210	187	122
PAR:	3	3	3	3
HDCP:	12	12	12	16

17

Even George Washington would use an extra club to get the silver dollar over this river. This body of water may be only a lagoon, but it's still best to avoid it. Bunker short right is the least of your concerns. Playing the ball to the right side may be longer over the water, but the bunker and out-of-bounds to the left should be out of the way. A 3 is definitely admirable on this hole.

— 29
| 30

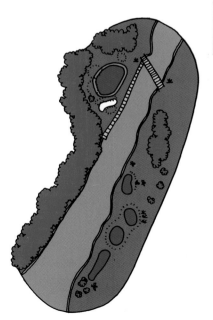

GEORGE FAZIO GOLF CLUB

18

	GOLD	BLUE	WHITE	RED
YDS:	462	445	424	350
PAR:	4	4	4	4
HDCP:	2	2	2	4

— 15
| 35

100 —

150 —

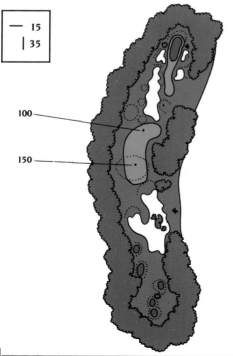

Still a few tricks left. The large bunker just off the tee is on the side of a hill. A blind drive is the result. This long finishing hole should not be taken for granted. Play the drive down the left center of the fairway. A long approach must be accurate to keep out of the bunkers all around the green. Careful selection of club and observation of pin position is important to avoid the long putts on the long narrow green.

GEORGE FAZIO GOLF CLUB

Palmetto Dunes Plantation
P.O. Box 5849
Hilton Head Island, SC 29938
803-785-1138
Resort

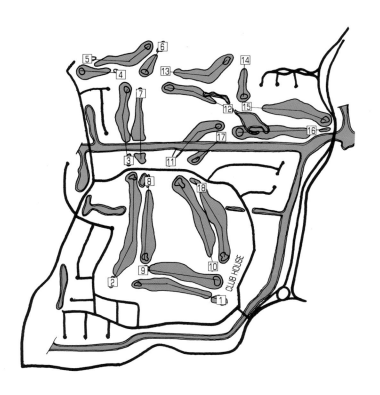

Course	Rating	Slope
Gold	74.2	132
Blue	72.6	126
White	71.2	123
Red	69.2	117

Director of Golf: Chip Pellerin
Head Professional: Billy Layman
Superintendent: Bill Elliot
Designer: George Fazio

HOLE	1	2	3	4	5	6	7	8	9	OUT	10	11	12	13	14	15	16	17	18	IN	TOTAL
GOLD	432	562	412	205	389	180	414	431	421	3446	513	394	387	386	185	445	425	230	462	3427	6873
BLUE	393	522	412	195	372	167	374	422	409	3266	513	376	364	366	164	414	416	210	445	3268	6534
WHITE	385	487	396	190	364	156	359	421	385	3143	485	364	319	354	150	410	403	187	424	3096	6239
HDCP	3	11	9	15	7	17	5	1	13		18	10	14	8	16	6	4	12	2		
PAR	4	5	4	3	4	3	4	4	4	35	5	4	4	4	3	4	4	3	4	35	70
RED	355	412	357	137	295	136	320	342	321	2675	438	320	275	279	123	342	349	122	350	2598	5273
HDCP	5	1	11	15	13	17	9	3	7		2	10	12	14	18	6	8	16	4		

The Course

Opened for play in 1969, the Robert Trent Jones course is one of the original courses on the island. The architect, Robert Trent Jones, designed the golf course making use of the interconnecting lagoon system within Palmetto Dunes. Water is present on eleven of the eighteen holes but is much more intrusive on the tenth than on all the rest. Straight out into the ocean, the tenth not only affords a magnificent view, but also a true test to the golfer. The wide-open fairways and spacious greens make the Jones course a pure pleasure to play.

The two holes starting the course are simply straight away. Gentle rolling of the fairway leads the golfer to the green. Conservative and smart play will keep the scores low. Mr. Jones leaves it up to the golfer to seize his/her own opportunities. The holes are not too long and only require the golfer to keep the ball in the fairway. The large greens are mostly flat. However, the bold putter may want to be cautious where putting surfaces slope downhill. These make up for the lack of water on the back nine.

Overconfidence will cause many to have problems on the tenth hole. At 540 yards, this par 5 plays straight out to the Atlantic, and strong onshore breezes can be expected. Sometimes even three solid hits will not reach this green. In that case, play the hole as a par 6 . . . and birdie it! Keeping the ball dry on the journey back to the clubhouse may prove to be tough, although the holes do get a little shorter.

Robert T. Jones has designed a course that provides not only an enjoyable round of golf, but also some very spectacular views. The Jones course is one to be thoroughly enjoyed.

ROBERT T. JONES COURSE

	BLUE	WHITE	RED
YDS:	400	390	342
PAR:	4	4	4
HDCP:	1	1	11

1

Mr. Jones starts off easy for the first hole. Wide open fairway invites the long drive. Play the ball down the right side for position. The elevated green is surrounded by three bunkers. The putts should drop on this hole.

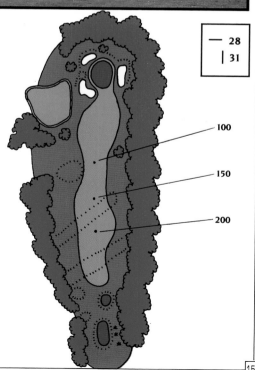

— 28
| 31

100

150

200

	BLUE	WHITE	RED
YDS:	383	364	350
PAR:	4	4	4
HDCP:	5	5	5

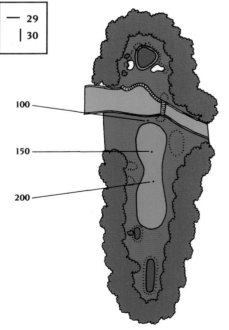

— 29
| 30

100

150

200

Length is not a factor on this second hole. However, the lagoon that crosses the fairway may be. The right side of the fairway is favored. Be sure to use the correct club on the approach shot. The large undulating green is a welcome haven beyond the water hazard.

ROBERT T. JONES COURSE

	BLUE	WHITE	RED
YDS:	361	342	319
PAR:	4	4	4
HDCP:	9	9	7

3

The drive off the tee can be tight. This third hole bends around to the right. Keep the ball in the center of the fairway. It is advised that you avoid the large bunkers on the right. The bunker front left makes the green appear small and difficult. But don't be fooled. There's a lot of room up there.
Play for the center. Two putts and a par — not bad.

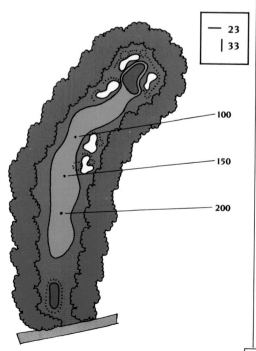

— 23
| 33

100

150

200

ROBERT T. JONES COURSE

4

	BLUE	WHITE	RED
YDS:	539	507	461
PAR:	5	5	5
HDCP:	7	7	3

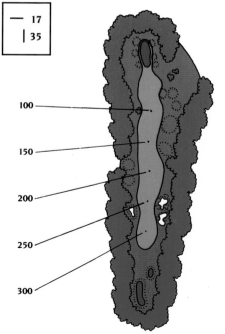

— 17
| 35

100

150

200

250

300

Fairway bunkers are the only sand on this hole. They can be passed on the drive. Play a little Army golf here — left off the tee, right on the second, and back left on the approach. Note the long, narrow green.

ROBERT T. JONES COURSE

	BLUE	WHITE	RED
YDS:	201	159	113
PAR:	3	3	3
HDCP:	17	17	17

5

The view from this tee clues you into the vast amount sand around the green. This is the longest par 3 on the course. If this hole can be completed successfully, the remaining 3's should be easy. Right? Prevailing wind is from the right, so keep it right and let the breeze push the ball back on course. If no wind, go for the stick! These four bunkers are also best avoided.

— 28
| 33

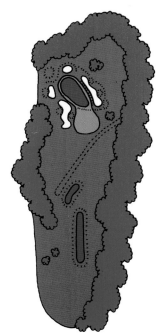

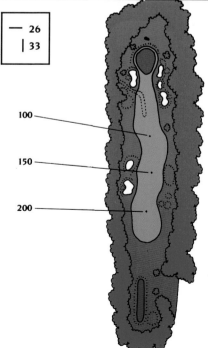

— 26
| 33

100
150
200

This is not the place to play a third shot. The second should be on the green! Actually this sixth hole is very demanding. The tee shot should be played down the right side, leaving a good angle to the putting surface. The large green slopes foward; three putts are possible, though not advised!

ROBERT T. JONES COURSE

	BLUE	WHITE	RED
YDS:	401	378	361
PAR:	4	4	4
HDCP:	11	11	9

7

This wide open fairway can be deceiving. Fairway bunkers left and mounding to the right will rightfully direct your attention to the center. Play the drive good and strong down the middle. Into the wind, this hole can be long. Get the approach close.

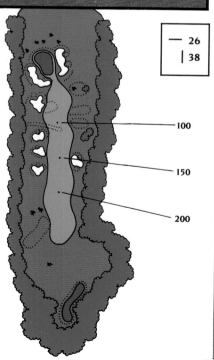

— 26
| 38

100

150

200

	BLUE	WHITE	RED
YDS:	198	159	92
PAR:	3	3	3
HDCP:	15	15	15

— 33
| 22

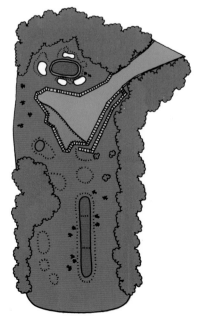

The wall bordering the water only adds to the severity of the scenery. And four bunkers surround the green, as if the water weren't enough! The green is wider than it is long. Club selection and shot are important. Be careful of the wind.

The front nine does not give up easily. Jones has brought in the length of a par 5, some water — and added a dogleg — just to make it interesting. Keeping the ball left is imperative. The lagoon veers in too much and far too long to cut across, and the wind is usually blowing left to right.

The large green is elevated and well protected by bunkers. Birdies are nice, but pars are respectable.

The front is now behind you; the back nine is next. And, take our word, it's best to be in good spirits for the next hole.

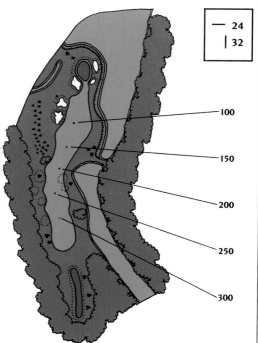

— 24
| 32

100

150

200

250

300

ROBERT T. JONES COURSE

10

	BLUE	WHITE	RED
YDS:	540	482	433
PAR:	5	5	5
HDCP:	10	10	2

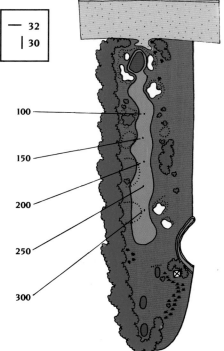

How can a hole so beautiful be so difficult? Well, because of the yardage, for one thing. Into the wind, even the best three shots may not be enough. The breeze off the ocean can be fierce!

Fairway bunkers right indicate the left side of the fairway is the target. The second should be played down the right. Once on the green, take a look out toward the beach. Breathtaking! Sometimes the scenery is better than the golf.

ROBERT T. JONES COURSE

	BLUE	WHITE	RED	11
YDS:	376	347	242	
PAR:	4	4	4	
HDCP:	8	8	14	

A long drive is to be expected when the wind is blowing down this hole. The large, round green is receptive to accurate second shots. Birdies are in the air, and after the last hole, they're welcome! Note the creek that wraps around the green to the lagoon on the left.

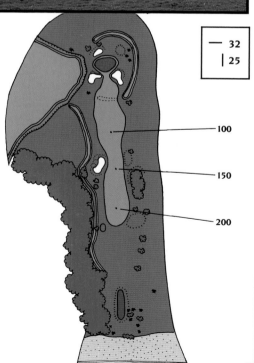

— 32
| 25

100

150

200

— 29
| 30

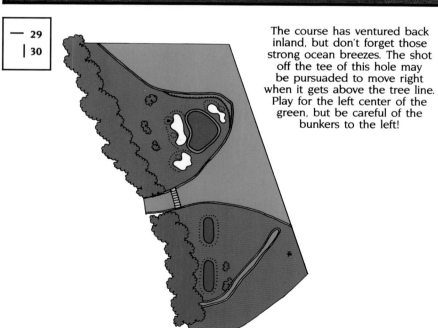

The course has ventured back inland, but don't forget those strong ocean breezes. The shot off the tee of this hole may be pursuaded to move right when it gets above the tree line. Play for the left center of the green, but be careful of the bunkers to the left!

ROBERT T. JONES COURSE

	BLUE	WHITE	RED
YDS:	380	283	256
PAR:	4	4	4
HDCP:	14	14	10

13

Playing amid all the water should have become second nature by now. This thirteenth is not long, but it does require control off the tee. From the center of the fairway, the approach is to a strangely shaped green which is well protected by bunkers. Note the location of the flag and play accordingly.

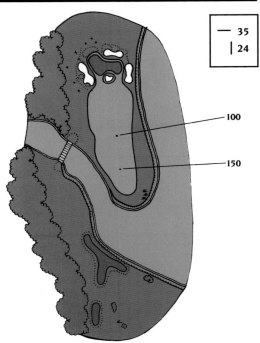

ROBERT T. JONES COURSE

14

	BLUE	WHITE	RED
YDS:	417	385	359
PAR:	4	4	4
HDCP:	2	2	12

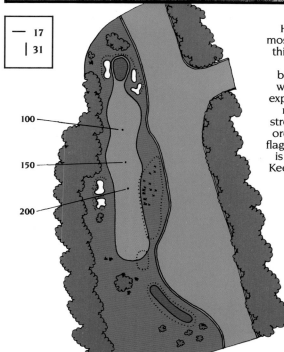

— 17
| 31

100
150
200

Handicapped as the second most difficult hole on this course, this par 4 lives up to its rating. Water down the right and bunkers left leave the middle wide open! Actually, the right expands, so the drive should be more to the right center. A strong approach is necessary in order to get the ball up to the flag. The elevated putting surface is bordered by three bunkers. Keep your short game polished.

ROBERT T. JONES COURSE

	BLUE	WHITE	RED
YDS:	506	488	460
PAR:	5	5	5
HDCP:	12	12	4

15

The largest green on the course awaits. The water still laps along the right side. Play the drive down the left side. The second shot should be followed down the right center. Bunkers and mounding surround the green.

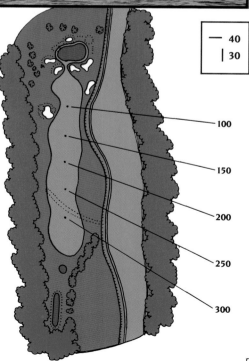

— 40
| 30

100

150

200

250

300

ROBERT T. JONES COURSE

16

	BLUE	WHITE	RED
YDS:	378	350	323
PAR:	4	4	4
HDCP:	6	6	8

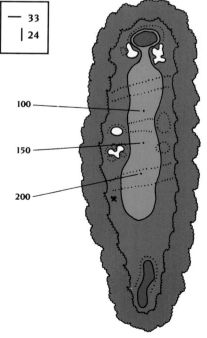

Back into the woods and away from the water. This sixteenth par 4 is not long, but it's difficult. Drive the ball down the right side to avoid the bunkers to the left. The mounding along the right will help direct the tee shot back into the center of the fairway. The approach is to a very tight green. Two bunkers front the green, while a wall of trees borders the back.

ROBERT T. JONES COURSE

	BLUE	WHITE	RED
YDS:	179	156	91
PAR:	3	3	3
HDCP:	16	16	18

17

The tee is deep within the trees in a jungle-like setting. One bunker left and two right will tighten the grip. Relax and just knock the ball up to the center of the green and don't even be concerned with the water hazard that wraps around the green.

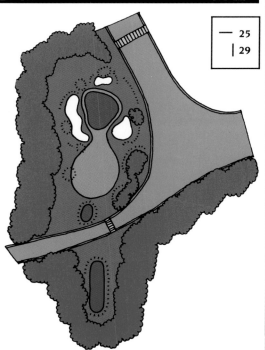

— 25
| 29

171

ROBERT T. JONES COURSE

18

	BLUE	WHITE	RED
YDS:	390	366	337
PAR:	4	4	4
HDCP:	4	4	6

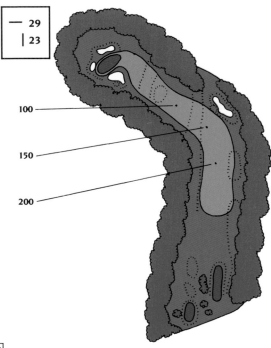

— 29
| 23

100

150

200

Almost back to the clubhouse, but Jones still has one more hole to keep you honest. The dogleg to the left will be the test. The fairway bunker on the right side is the target off the tee. An elevated green is surrounded by bunkers is the finish line. Keep the approach to the right side in order to avoid this large bunker. Give the crowd at the clubhouse a good show! Birdie this eighteenth!

ROBERT T. JONES COURSE

Palmetto Dunes Plantation
P.O. Box 5849
Hilton Head Island, SC 29938
803-785-1136
Resort

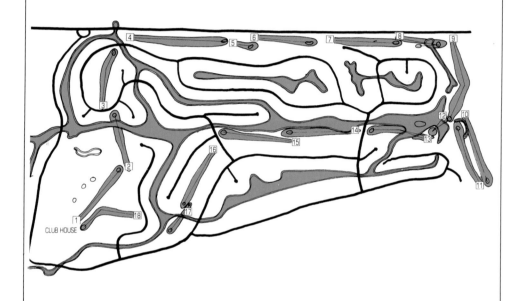

Course	Rating	Slope
Blue	72.2	123
White	69.3	119
Red	70.7	117

Director of Golf: Chip Pellerin
Head Professional: Clark Sinclair
Superintendent: John Betts
Designer: Robert Trent Jones

HOLE	1	2	3	4	5	6	7	8	9	OUT	10	11	12	13	14	15	16	17	18	IN	TOTAL
BLUE	400	383	361	539	201	397	401	198	510	3390	540	376	154	380	417	506	378	179	390	3320	6710
WHITE	390	364	342	507	159	371	378	159	483	3153	482	347	138	283	385	488	350	156	366	2995	6148
HDCP	1	5	9	7	17	3	11	15	13		10	8	18	14	2	12	6	16	4		
PAR	4	4	4	5	3	4	4	3	5	36	5	4	3	4	3	5	4	3	4	36	72
RED	342	350	319	461	113	340	361	92	444	2822	433	242	102	256	359	460	323	91	337	2603	5425
HDCP	11	5	7	3	17	13	9	15	1		2	14	16	10	12	4	8	18	6		

PALMETTO HALL PLANTATION

The Plantation

The newest plantation, as of this publication date, on Hilton Head Island. Boasting two new eighteen-hole layouts, Palmetto Hall is the second smallest plantation on the island, with only 750 acres. Surprisingly, though, the two courses are each over 6900 yards. The Hills course measures a total of 6918 yards and is scheduled to be open for play in March 1991. The second course, designed by Robert Cupp, will be over 7100 yards and will open for play around 1993. This will then be the longest golf course on Hilton Head Island.

HILLS GOLF COURSE

Palmetto Hall Plantation
Hilton Head Island, SC

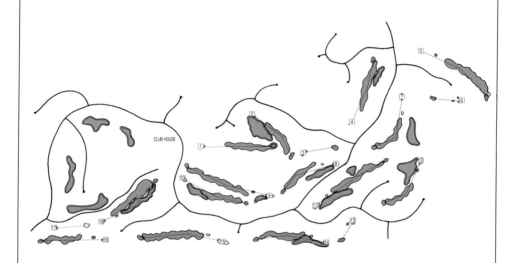

CLUB HOUSE

Designer: Arthur Hills

HOLE	1	2	3	4	5	6	7	8	9	OUT	10	11	12	13	14	15	16	17	18	IN	TOTAL
GOLD	438	395	192	437	490	191	397	382	546	3468	398	526	378	158	442	521	403	190	434	3450	6918
BLUE	420	385	186	407	472	170	383	366	525	3314	381	513	347	151	424	500	360	161	411	3268	6582
WHITE	405	371	171	375	461	148	367	354	501	3153	371	491	328	133	412	472	365	143	389	3104	6257
PAR	4	4	3	4	5	3	4	4	5	36	4	5	4	3	4	5	4	3	4	36	72
RED	334	241	75	270	360	121	302	296	425	2444	302	411	231	104	338	404	320	99	303	2512	4956

PORT ROYAL PLANTATION

The Plantation

Port Royal offers the only private oceanside community on Hilton Head Island. The famed racquet club features many tennis courts as well as all three tennis surfaces. The plantation also includes two championship croquet courts. The scenic area is a treasure trove of history, much of which is summarized on the tee markers on each of the three championship golf courses. The golf courses include:

Barony Golf Course

Planter's Row Golf Course

Robber's Row Golf Course

The Course

Opened for play in 1963, the Barony golf course is a solid golf course. Fairways are open and yet require positioning off the tee in order to reach the greens in regulation. The putting surfaces are small and tricky. Large, deep bunkers surround the putting surfaces, greedily snagging any stray shots. The length of the course is comfortable at a little over 6500 yards. George Cobb and Willard Byrd have produced a golf course which will put all shots of the game to the test.

A wide-open fairway greets the golfer on the first tee. A casual drive, preferably down the left middle, will get the game started. The large green leads the golfer to believe that this is going to be an easy day — that is, until the second hole, which is a par 3. The third stretches into a par 5 around a corner. Two easy shots will set up the approach, which is to a very small green surrounded by bunkers. Once past the first three holes, the rest of the front is routine — good solid drives followed by crisp iron shots to the hearts of the greens. Complete the front with a good score to keep up the momentum going into the more difficult back nine.

The tenth hole is a short dogleg wrapped around a large pond. The tee shot is a tangent off the edge of the water, setting up a good angle on the approach to a putting surface that appears to be cut right into the water. The long eleventh hole requires conservative par 5 procedures. The thirteenth is short and interesting, having a green hidden in the trees. The fifteenth is the shortest par 5 on the course, so getting home in two is not an unreasonable ambition.

George Cobb and Willard Byrd have teamed up to design an excellent golf course that requires more control than just the ability to hit the ball far. This opening hole is true to form. A short, accurate drive is necessary to position the ball for the approach.

The approach, best from the left side of the fairway, must stay well away from the water hazard short left and keep out of the three bunkers surrounding the green.

This first green slopes rather quickly toward the front. Beyond the hole, downhill putts are slippery. You'll have a solid uphill putt from below.

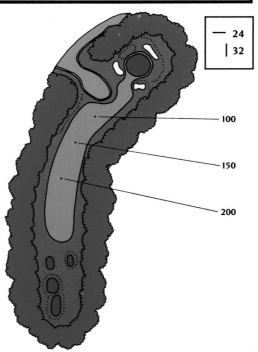

— 24
| 32

100

150

200

2

	BLUE	WHITE	RED
YDS:	185	155	127
PAR:	3	3	3
HDCP:	13	13	13

— 31
| 30

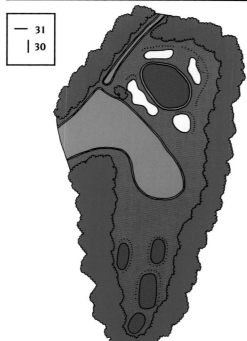

This par 3 can be a quick play. Par 3 is always acceptable on shorter holes like this, but attempting a birdie can be risky, leading to a bitter end. Play smart and conservatively. The birdies will come!

It is imperative to hit the ball long enough on this tee shot. Any shots without enough distance will end up in the water. If that is not pressure enough, take a good look at the four bunkers that corner the putting surface. The best way to play the hole is to simply hit the tee shot to the center of the green, two putts and par, and on to the next hole!

BARONY GOLF COURSE

	BLUE	WHITE	RED
YDS:	523	475	418
PAR:	5	5	5
HDCP:	7	7	5

3

This third hole bends elusively to the left. The wide fairway is unbiased to the driver. Either a right or a left will put you in a good position for a second shot, but the right side of the fairway gives a better view down the fairway.

The second shot is also of little concern, only that it remain in the fairway and be moved forward!

The green is well protected by bunkers. The approach should be made to the center of the green. There are just too many bunkers around to risk a tricky shot to a tough pin placement. The putting surface slopes slowly toward the front of the green.

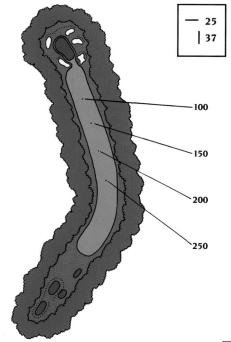

BARONY GOLF COURSE

4

	BLUE	WHITE	RED
YDS:	382	354	311
PAR:	4	4	4
HDCP:	1	1	1

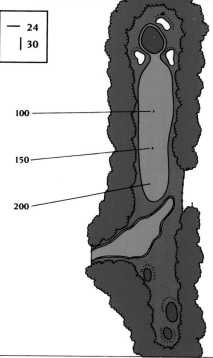

— 24
| 30

100

150

200

The tees are elevated, giving a good view of the fairway. A strong drive down the middle should set up perfectly for the approach. Don't disregard the wind here. A strong breeze above the tree line will push the ball off course.

The second shot is to a slightly elevated green which is protected by three bunkers. An auspicious hit will come to rest just inches from the cup.

BARONY GOLF COURSE

	BLUE	WHITE	RED
YDS:	362	323	301
PAR:	4	4	4
HDCP:	17	17	9

5

Short and straight-away They don't get any easier than this. The landing area is open for the big drive. However, the green comes with a few bunkers.

Play the drive down the right middle of the fairway. The second shot must keep well clear of the water hazard (short left) and the three bunkers fronting the green.

The putting surface is undulant. Gentle sloping towards the front right and left will test the authority of the putter.

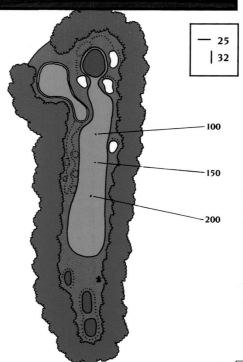

— 25
| 32

100

150

200

— 23
| 22

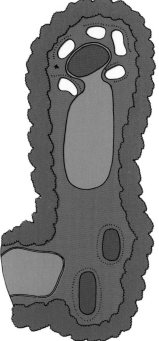

This par 3 is somewhat shorter than the first. Bunkers lie ominously awaiting their visitors. A strong tee shot to the center of the green must take into account the ever-present winds. The sloping green demands a delicate touch from the putter. Par will keep the competition in line.

BARONY GOLF COURSE

	BLUE	WHITE	RED
YDS:	375	347	317
PAR:	4	4	4
HDCP:	5	5	7

7

This seventh requires two solid shots to reach the green in regulation. Accuracy is a must off the tee and on the approach.

The tee shot should be played straight down the middle. There is no fairway bunker to find. Control is still necessary to keep clear of the trees right and left.

The green is elevated and surrounded by bunkers. Any deviation off course is sure to find the deep sandy pits. Once on the putting surface, however, the putts should drop easily.

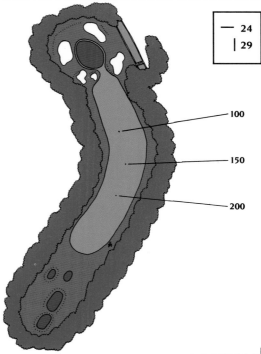

— 24
| 29

100

150

200

BARONY GOLF COURSE

8

	BLUE	WHITE	RED
YDS:	359	328	295
PAR:	4	4	4
HDCP:	9	9	15

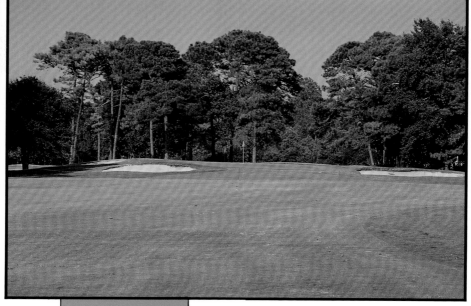

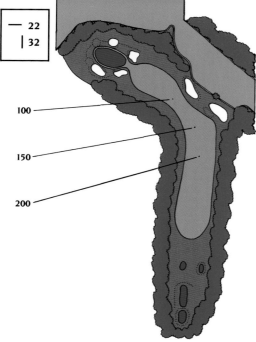

— 22
| 32

100
150
200

The eighth is very similar to the seventh. The dogleg wraps around to the left. Two fairway bunkers lurk in the distance. Care must be taken to get the ball down the left side of the fairway in optimal position to go for the green.

The approach should be directed to the center of the green. The frontward sloping surface will make for very slippery downhill putts if the ball is hit past the hole. Putts short of the hole can be stroked with confidence.

9

The ninth has been designed as a par 5. The front nine is completed with length. The hole starts off simply and straight-away, but then turns sharply to the left near the end. Two well hit shots will leave a fairly short shot to be played over the corner to the well bunkered green.

A mighty drive straight down the middle is the most desirable approach. Bunker and water will be the fate of balls hit too far to the right. Menacing trees line the left side.

The second shot must be played down the right side in order to set up a good angle on the approach. The third shot may be from past the corner, thus establishing an open path to the putting surface. Those who do not get the second that far will have to gently loft the approach over the corner onto the green. The small green will keep the game interesting.

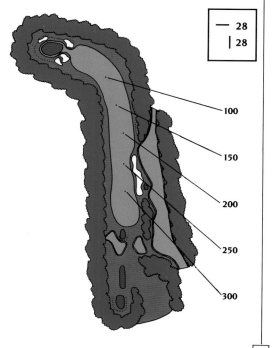

— 28
| 28

100

150

200

250

300

	BLUE	WHITE	RED
YDS:	337	329	286
PAR:	4	4	4
HDCP:	6	6	12

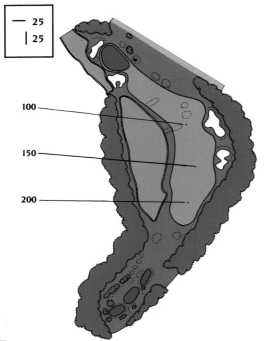

— 25
| 25

100

150

200

The course designers have given us a break — a short easy hole to begin the back nine.

It's more important to position the drive off the tee than to try for a long hit. Water is ever-present along the left side, while two bunkers lie in wait on the far side of the dogleg. The drive should be no longer than 200 yards, aimed just left of the first bunker on the right.

The approach can be touchy. Bunkers and water on the left are incentives to keep the shots right. A pin placed on the front left corner of the green is nearly impossible to reach on the approach.

BARONY GOLF COURSE

	BLUE	WHITE	RED	11
YDS:	538	507	400	
PAR:	5	5	5	
HDCP:	8	8	8	

Whereas the tenth was the shortest hole on the course, the eleventh is the longest. A par 5, double dogleg, this hole is critical. A mighty drive is a must in order to get the ball in position for a second shot that will be able to clear the water. The third shot must be accurate and find its way up to the green.

Play the drive, as far as possible, down the left side of the fairway. Be careful not to roll into the water that follows up the left side. The second shot should be aimed at the palm tree which sits in the middle of the fairway, about 150 yards out.

The approach must avoid the three greenside bunkers. The wind will pick up just around the last dogleg into the green. Note the direction and velocity of the breeze and play accordingly. Birdies will keep the competition at bay.

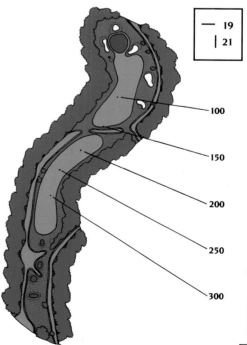

— 19
| 21

100

150

200

250

300

12

	BLUE	WHITE	RED
YDS:	428	396	363
PAR:	4	4	4
HDCP:	2	2	4

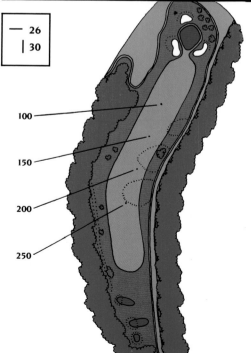

— 26
| 30

100
150
200
250

The twelfth stretches out to become the longest par 4 on the course. A strong drive down the left middle of the fairway will keep the ball well clear of the water on the right and will open the view to the green.

The wind is a big factor on this hole, since it heads directly out toward the ocean. A long approach can be expected. Be sure to use enough club to get the ball onto the center of the green, in position for the par.

The flat surface of the green will allow putts to roll true and save par. Bogeys on this hole are no discrace.

BARONY GOLF COURSE

	BLUE	WHITE	RED
YDS:	367	345	307
PAR:	4	4	4
HDCP:	12	12	6

13

Those who enjoy the big risk, and have the ability to hit the ball at least 300 yards on the fly, may want to try to go for this green from the tee! However, care must be taken. There could be an outcry from homeowners on the left side of the pond if the tee shot does not get up to the desired altitude and crashes into the side of a house!

The less adventurous would play their drive down the middle of the fairway, keeping well short of the fairway bunkers. A short approach would follow into the tight target area that is the green.

The long narrow putting surface is flat and receptive to accurate approach shots. Anything less than accurate will go into the trees or bunkers. A conservative par is advisable because of the trouble just waiting to plague you.

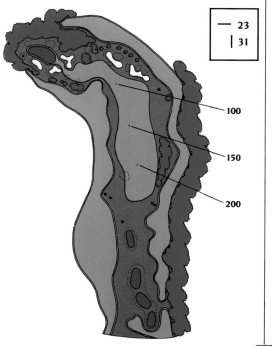

— 23
| 31

100

150

200

BARONY GOLF COURSE

14

	BLUE	WHITE	RED
YDS:	153	134	107
PAR:	3	3	3
HDCP:	18	18	16

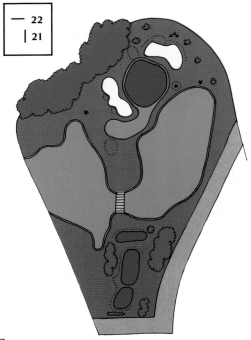

— 22
| 21

While the tee is tucked in amongst the pines and protected from the strong ocean breezes, the green is open and unprotected. Care must be taken to avoid having the ball pushed off line by the wind.

The large round putting surface is an easy target from the tee. Plan on two putts. Par, or even bogey, are good scores on this hole.

	BLUE	WHITE	RED
YDS:	480	463	374
PAR:	5	5	5
HDCP:	16	16	10

Two solid shots should be enough to reach this green. The fairway is relatively wide open, giving a good target to aim for from the tee. Water comes in, periodically, from the left. Except for one lone pine, standing tall in the middle of the fairway, there are not any obstructions between the tee and green.

The tee shot should be aimed just left of the tree in the middle of the fairway. This will keep the ball down the right middle of the fairway, opening up to a clear view of the green.

On the second shot, follow with a big hit directly for the green. If long enough, it should roll up to the flagstick. If not, the third shot will be short and easy.

The small putting surface slopes quickly toward the front. Take your time on the first putt and knock it into the hole for the birdie or, possibly, eagle!

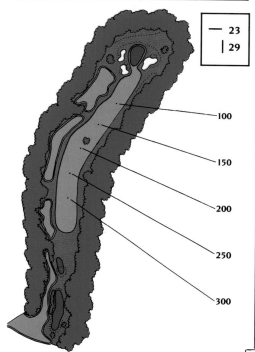

— 23
| 29

100

150

200

250

300

BARONY GOLF COURSE

16

	BLUE	WHITE	RED
YDS:	196	162	140
PAR:	3	3	3
HDCP:	14	14	18

26
29

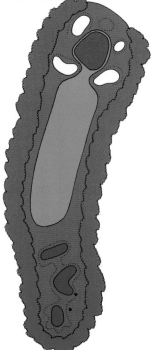

The second par 3 in only three holes! This sixteenth is quite long, measuring almost 200 yards from the back tees.

Bunkers provide plenty of intimidation for the tee shot. Play for the center of the green and accept any variation thereof. The putting surface is undulant. Putts can be tricky.

This seventeenth is a possible birdie hole. A good drive down the right middle will set up an easy approach. The wide green is flat and receptive to the well-hit second shot.

With the wind at your back, the desire to hit a big drive cannot be resisted. Go for it! Only a little bit of water is found, way over to the left. Keep your shot straight and there should not be any problems.

A solid shot at the flagstick should come to rest inches from the hole. Allow your competitor to "give" you the putt, mark down the birdie and step up to the next, final hole.

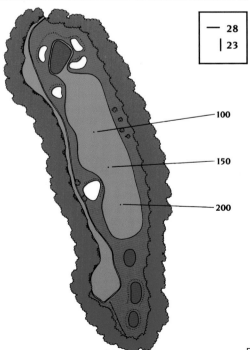

— 28
| 23

100

150

200

	BLUE	WHITE	RED
YDS:	405	385	351
PAR:	4	4	4
HDCP:	4	4	2

— 29
| 25

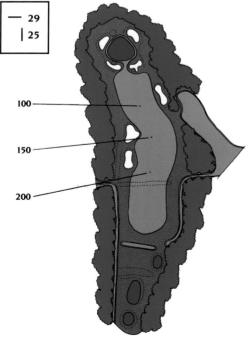

100

150

200

The designers have not let up for the eighteenth hole. A strong drive is a must to get the ball in good position for the approach.

Water and bunkers have been added, making the drive a bit tense. Aim the tee shot to the right of the bunkers, placing the ball on the left side of the fairway. A medium-length second shot is to a green that is well protected by bunkers.

The putting surface slopes to both sides. The needed one putt must be well surveyed before knocking into it the hole.

BARONY GOLF COURSE

Port Royal Plantation
P.O. Drawer 7229
Hilton Head Island, SC 29938
803-681-3671
Resort

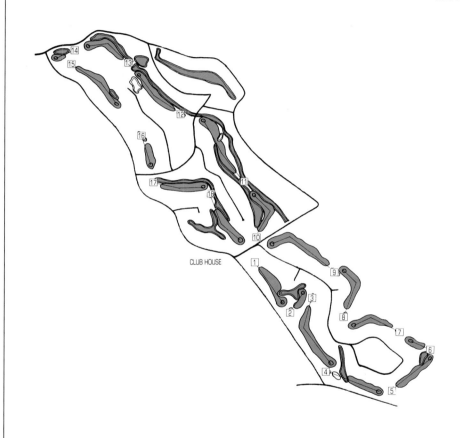

Course	Rating	Slope
Blue	71.2	124
White	69.2	122
Red	70.1	115

Head Professional: Gary Duren
Superintendent: David DeGeorge
Designers: George Cobb & Willard Byrd
Teaching Professional: Keith Marks, Sr.

HOLE	1	2	3	4	5	6	7	8	9	OUT	10	11	12	13	14	15	16	17	18	IN	TOTAL
BLUE	365	185	523	382	362	174	375	359	533	3258	337	538	428	367	153	480	196	368	405	3272	6530
WHITE	336	155	475	354	323	164	347	328	490	2972	329	507	396	345	134	463	162	345	385	3066	6038
HDCP	15	13	7	1	17	11	5	9	3		6	8	2	12	18	16	14	10	4		
PAR	4	3	5	4	4	3	4	4	5	36	4	5	4	4	3	5	3	4	4	36	72
RED	290	127	418	311	301	132	317	295	432	2623	286	400	363	307	107	374	140	302	351	2630	5253
HDCP	11	13	5	1	9	17	7	15	3		12	8	4	6	16	10	18	14	2		

The Course

This course was designed by Willard Byrd and opened for play in 1984. Planter's Row is the newest and the shortest of the three Port Royal courses. The course has enjoyed such notability as hosting the 1985 Hilton Head Seniors International Tournament. Parallel tree-lined fairways set the course apart from the others on the island. Rolling fairways are played up to large, undulating greens which require a confident putter indeed. Water sneaks into the scene on many holes, but carefully executed golf shots should be able to keep the ball in play and provide an enjoyable round.

The front nine leads the golfer away from the clubhouse into a park-like setting where the eighteen holes are laid out. Once the course heads out, it does not return to the clubhouse until the eighteenth hole. The first few holes will test the controllabilty of the driver and the accuracy of the approach shot. The first glimpse of water is on the par 3 fourth hole, and the fifth, with water present over 90% of the way, is sure to claim a few balls. Use the front nine as a warm up, for the back, where the holes become more difficult.

A straightaway par 4 opens up the second nine. Fairway bunkers are utilized with more frequency. Straight drives are a must to set up for the long approaches on most of the holes. The twelfth hole is the longest par 4 at 424 yards. Planter's Row finishes strong with a par 5 at 552, yards requiring all that you have got — and then some!

The first hole of the Planters Row course starts the round off rather simply. Only one lone bunker is found along the left side of the fairway. An oak protrudes from the right side, steering the drives towards the left.

The drive must be played straight down the center of the fairway, accented with a slight fade. Mounding along the right will push balls back to the center.

The green is small with slight sloping. An approach should avoid the grass bunker front right. Be advised that the mounding near the green gives the illusion that the green is farther away than it actually is. A par will start the day off right.

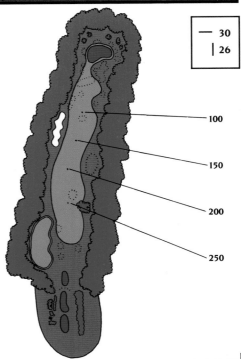

— 30
| 26

100

150

200

250

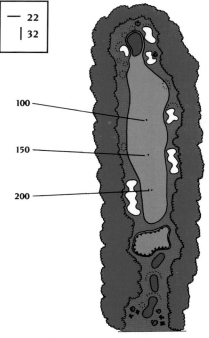

— 22
| 32

100

150

200

The second hole requires a carry over a water hazard to a fairway that is slightly elevated. Fairway bunkers must also be avoided. The tree-lined fairway necessitates control from tee to green.

The approach to a level green is not too long, so here's a grand opportunity for a birdie. Use a clean, crisp, short iron for the hit right to the cup. A few undulations will add a test of your putting ability. However, the approach that comes to rest near the hole should be knocked in without problems.

This third hole is only slightly longer than the second. A water hazard runs the entire length of the hole along the right side. The large fairway bunker on the right can be reached with a long drive.

A medium approach shot should be played to a long green. But beware! The three bunkers surrounding the putting surface will catch any errant tee shots.

Once on the green, longer putts should be lagged up close to the hole, eliminating the possiblity of three putts. Par will keep pace with the competition.

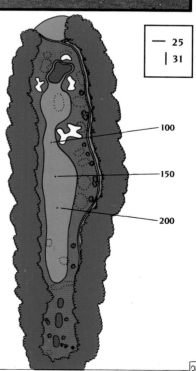

— 25
| 31

100

150

200

PLANTER'S ROW GOLF COURSE

4

	BLUE	WHITE	RED
YDS:	157	136	109
PAR:	3	3	3
HDCP:	17	17	15

— 24

| 31

This first par three is not too long. A water hazard sits well short of the putting surface, while two bunkers lie ominously in front. The large putting area is flat, providing a good surface for chances at the birdies.

Longer hitters will be able to get to this green in two. But the second water hazard may also be reachable from the tee. The conservative player should hit the drive directly down the middle, staying left of the fairway bunkers on the right.

A strong second shot may be required to clear the second hazard and set up for the approach.

The green is tucked in beyond a bunker on the left. The right side of the fairway slopes down from the right. Accuracy is a must to get the ball close to the hole. The putting surface slopes to the right.

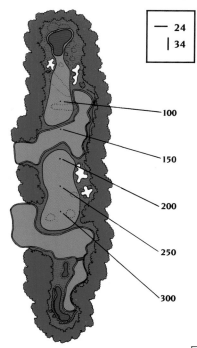

— 24
| 34

100

150

200

250

300

PLANTER'S ROW GOLF COURSE

6

	BLUE	WHITE	RED
YDS:	161	146	101
PAR:	3	3	3
HDCP:	15	15	17

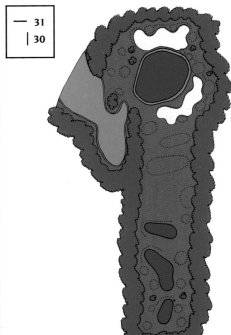

— 31
| 30

This sixth is just a bit longer than the fourth. A solid tee shot to the left center of the green will assure safety from the bunkers, short and long.

The large undulating putting surface slopes left. Tricky sidehill, downhill, and even uphill putts can be expected unless the tee shot nestles up close to the pin.

The trees are overpowering from the right. A strong drive down the right middle of the fairway will set up optimal position for the approach. A fairway wood or long iron may provide better precision off the tee.

The second shot to the green must dodge bunkers which are short left and long right. The putting surface is flat and receptive to the strong approach.

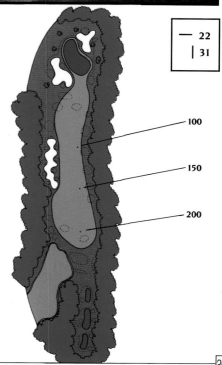

— 22
| 31

100

150

200

PLANTER'S ROW GOLF COURSE

8

	BLUE	WHITE	RED
YDS:	391	365	309
PAR:	4	4	4
HDCP:	7	7	11

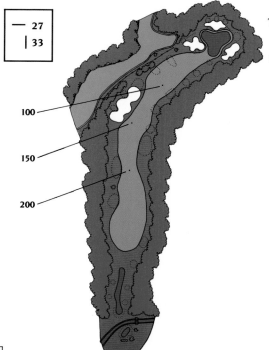

— 27
| 33

100

150

200

This eighth is the second longest par 4 on the front side. The drive can be tricky. The player must keep the ball left and long enough to get around the corner. However, the bunker on the far side of the dogleg will attract shots that are too long.

The approach must be hit to the center of the green in order to get the easy par.

PLANTER'S ROW GOLF COURSE

	BLUE	WHITE	RED
YDS:	510	480	437
PAR:	5	5	5
HDCP:	5	5	3

9

The ninth finishes with a medium-length par 5. Water sneaks in from the left side as you get near the green. Three well-planned shots should get the ball up on the green and in position for the birdie.

The drive must be down the left center of the fairway, keeping clear of the fairway bunker right and the water to the left. The second shot follows, delicately, down the center. A short approach is to a small flat putting surface.

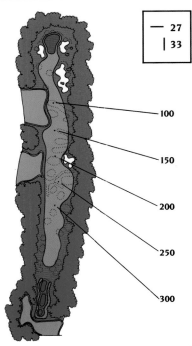

— 27
| 33

100

150

200

250

300

10

	BLUE	WHITE	RED
YDS:	361	330	285
PAR:	4	4	4
HDCP:	14	14	16

— 22
| 37

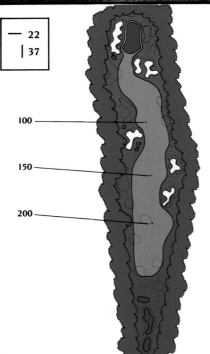

100
150
200

The tenth requires position from the tee. Two bunkers right and one bunker left will snag any shots hit off line. The drive must be played just left of the first bunker on the left. (However, the drive must not find the bunker on the left.)

From the fairway, the approach is to a green which is tucked in behind two bunkers right middle. Accuracy is important. The undulating green will add dimension for the bold putter.

The holes begin to run parallel to each other. This eleventh requires a slight fade off the tee to avoid the fairway bunker on the left. Water dabbles within the first 150 yards, but this shouldn't be of great concern. The second shot must circumnavigate bunkers to find the green.

The putting surface slopes slowly toward the front. The putter will be most appreciated upon sinking the long downhill putt.

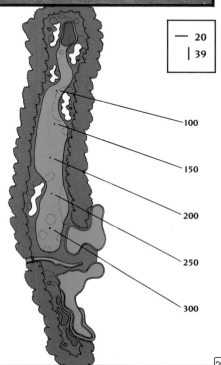

| — 20 |
| \| 39 |

100

150

200

250

300

	BLUE	WHITE	RED
YDS:	424	395	332
PAR:	4	4	4
HDCP:	2	2	2

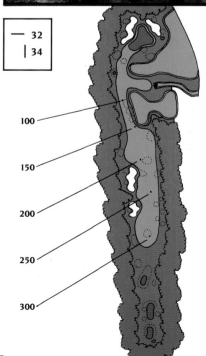

This par 4 stretches out a bit. A smashing drive down the center is a must to get within comfortable range of the green. The pines are ever-present right and left, producing a tight and narrow fairway. The approach to the green must clear not only one body of water, but two! An accurate shot will be vital if the decision has been to lay up.

The water wraps around to the right, penalizing shots that miss the green to that side. Bunkers left and beyond cover the remaining sides. The putting surface slopes away from the water. Par is admirable here, bogey is common.

The water peeks in on the right side briefly by the tee and once again nearer the green. A long bunker expands down the left side of the fairway. A powerful drive along the right middle of the fairway will set up well for the approach.

The second shot into the green must be played to the center. Careful! The wind picks up over the water, pushing a seemingly well-hit shot off line. Keep the putt on main street and watch it fall into the cup.

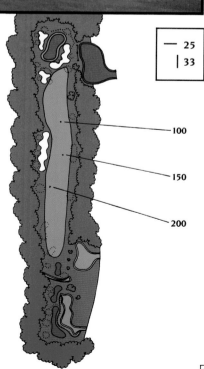

— 25
| 33

—100

—150

—200

PLANTER'S ROW GOLF COURSE

14

	BLUE	WHITE	RED
YDS:	377	351	317
PAR:	4	4	4
HDCP:	10	10	8

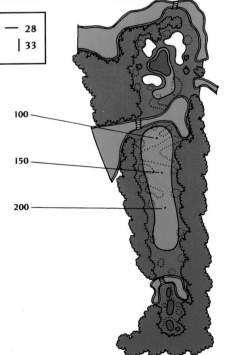

— 28
| 33

100

150

200

The last few holes have mandated length as well as control. This fourteenth reduces the yardage a bit. Accuracy and position, however, are still a must.

The drive should be played down the right center of the fairway. Positioning is key. A fairway wood or even long iron might be the best choice for the job.

The approach is from about 135 yards from the green. The water should not present a problem — unless the ball flies undesirably. The putting surface is lowest in the center. Go for it!

PLANTER'S ROW GOLF COURSE

	BLUE	WHITE	RED
YDS:	173	144	112
PAR:	3	3	3
HDCP:	16	16	18

15

Swirling winds can add uncertainty to how this hole should be played. The green is placed delicately among bunkers and water. The putting surface slopes gradually toward the front. Length as well as accuracy are a must. Play the tee shot to the right side of the green, bringing it left as appropriate.

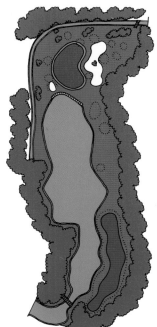

— 24
| 33

— 22
| 39

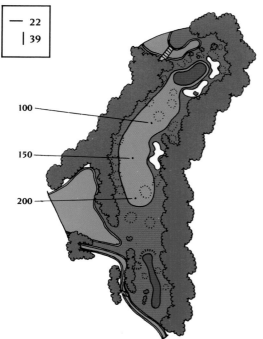

100

150

200

This sixteenth is a nice short par 4. Birdies are in the air. A drive straight down the center will set up the perfect angle for the approach. Beware of the water to the left and bunker to the right.

The fairway is slightly higher than the green, allowing for good visibilty of the putting surface. With the green also sloping toward the front, a tight approach shot is all but a formality. The birdie will keep the competition in the wake.

PLANTER'S ROW GOLF COURSE

	BLUE	WHITE	RED	
YDS:	184	161	125	**17**
PAR:	3	3	3	
HDCP:	18	18	14	

The longest par 3 on the course. With a prevailing headwind, this hole can be tough. The small green is wedged in among bunkers and trees. The tree to the right of the green may deflect a shot carving in from the right. Be sure to use more than enough club to reach the putting surface safely.

— 23
| 34

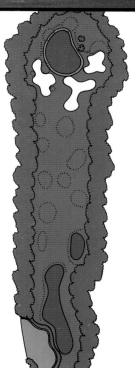

PLANTER'S ROW GOLF COURSE

18

	BLUE	WHITE	RED
YDS:	552	480	433
PAR:	5	5	5
HDCP:	4	4	4

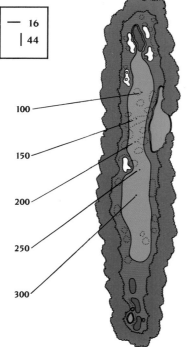

— 16
| 44

100
150
200
250
300

Willard Byrd has incorporated his whole bag of tricks into this lengthy finishing hole. A mighty drive will definitely improve the situation. The first fairway bunker on the left will grab those who stray too close. Water along the right will gladly accept the shots that slide right.

The elevated green is encircled by deep bunkers. Saving par from the sand is quite an accomplishment. Although a par would finish the day nicely, a bogey will not destroy the score.

PLANTER'S ROW GOLF CLUB

Port Royal Plantation
P.O. Drawer 7229
Hilton Head Island, SC 29938
803-681-3671
Resort

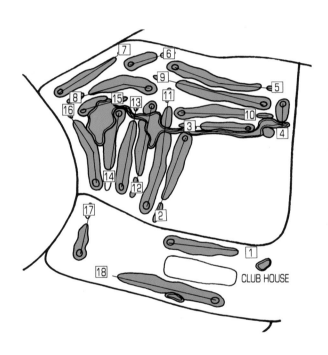

Course	Rating	Slope
Blue	72.1	128
White	70.6	126
Red	68.9	116

Head Professional: Gary Duren
Superintendent: David DeGeorge
Designer: Willard Byrd
Teaching Professional: Kieth Marks, Sr.

HOLE	1	2	3	4	5	6	7	8	9	OUT	10	11	12	13	14	15	16	17	18	IN	TOTAL
BLUE	399	336	352	157	505	161	345	391	510	3156	361	528	424	400	377	173	365	184	552	3364	6520
WHITE	363	326	336	136	475	146	327	365	480	2954	330	485	395	375	351	144	334	161	480	3055	6009
HDCP	3	9	11	17	1	15	13	7	5		14	6	2	8	10	16	12	18	4		
PAR	4	4	4	3	5	3	4	4	5	36	4	5	4	4	4	3	4	3	5	36	72
RED	327	289	283	109	387	101	271	309	437	2513	285	424	332	284	317	112	301	125	433	2613	5126
HDCP	5	7	9	15	1	17	13	11	3		16	6	2	12	8	18	10	14	4		

The Course

This course was designed by George Cobb and opened for play around 1963. One of Port Royal's three courses, this layout is built on a site once occupied as a strategic headquarters for many Civil War infantry units. While playing this course, the golfer is able to enjoy a great layout while learning about the Civil War times from the information provided on each tee marker. It's an educational experience that captures the interest of all who play the course. At more than 6700 yards, Robbers Row is a good test of the golfer's ability.

The front nine is shorter than the back. Starting with a dogleg par 4, measuring only 317 yards from the Blue tees, the first impression is that you're on an easy golf course. It is good to keep a positive attitude, but don't carried away. The second hole quickly stretches out to a 440-yard par 4! The rest of the nine is more in line with average-length holes. Only one par 5 is on the front, but be prepared to make up for this lack of par 5's on the back!

Where the front finished with a par of 35, the back includes a total of three par 5's to establish a total par of 37. The tenth hole can be called opportunity time. Its length will allow many to go for the green in two, while many more will happily play conservatively for the birdie. Mr. Byrd continues with an eleventh that checks in at 440 yards. Similar to the front, this side finishes with seven average-length holes. But the first two can catch many off guard.

ROBBER'S ROW COURSE

	BLUE	WHITE	RED
YDS:	317	296	264
PAR:	4	4	4
HDCP:	15	15	11

1

This first hole of Robber's Row seems very tight from the tee, but actually the landing area opens up for the drive. However, water does come in from the right, enough to cause anxious moments for those who hit the ball to the right.

The drive should be played down the left middle of the fairway, straight for the bunker on the left. An approach of about 120 yards can be expected into the green.

The green slopes slowly toward the front. A careful second shot should place the ball on the center of the putting surface. By relaxing and taking a good solid putt, par you can achieve par with no problem.

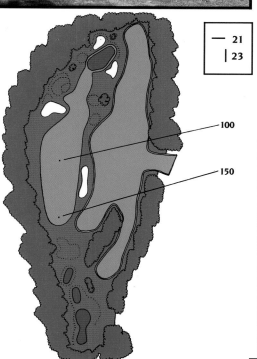

— 21
| 23

100

150

ROBBER'S ROW COURSE

2

	BLUE	WHITE	RED
YDS:	440	415	360
PAR:	4	4	4
HDCP:	3	3	5

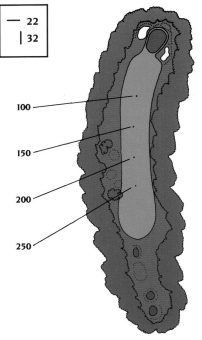

— 22
| 32

100
150
200
250

The second bends slightly to the right on a treelined fairway. There are no fairway bunkers to interfere on the way to the green, but the distance to the hole is quite long. A mighty drive down the middle is a must for a somewhat easy approach to the green.

The second shot must stay on course and avoid the greenside bunkers, left and right. The putting surface is flat at the back and slopes quickly to the front. Leave the ball short of the hole in order to have an easier uphill putt.

ROBBER'S ROW COURSE

	BLUE	WHITE	RED	
YDS:	407	364	334	**3**
PAR:	4	4	4	
HDCP:	7	7	3	

This par 4 tees off out of a funnel created by the trees on both sides. The elevated tees offer a good view of the hole.

The drive should be played down the right side, opening up the view to the green. The approach is to an elevated green fronted by a large bunker.

The putting surface slopes off to the right, making it alluring to hit the second shot to the right side of the green.

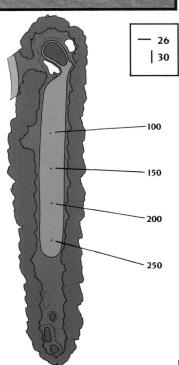

— 26
| 30

100

150

200

250

	BLUE	WHITE	RED
YDS:	199	175	148
PAR:	3	3	3
HDCP:	11	11	7

4

— 20
| 22

This fourth is open and long. The tee shot must find the elevated green and avoid falling short into the pond or bunkers, left and right.

Play the shot off the tee to the left center of the green, being careful not to pull it into the drink. (The prevailing winds are from the left).

The putting surface slopes drastically to the front. Any shots not up to the heart of the green can roll back down the front.

ROBBER'S ROW COURSE

	BLUE	WHITE	RED
YDS:	379	359	259
PAR:	4	4	4
HDCP:	9	9	13

5

The tee is situated behind a narrow gap that opens to the fairway. The drive must thread its way through the gap and down the right side.

The water comes in quite a way from the left — best to keep your distance. The second shot should be played from about 170 yards to the slightly elevated green, which is circled by bunkers.

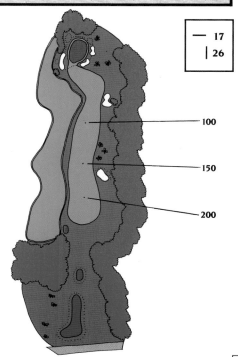

— 17
| 26

100

150

200

	BLUE	WHITE	RED
YDS:	564	527	456
PAR:	5	5	5
HDCP:	1	1	1

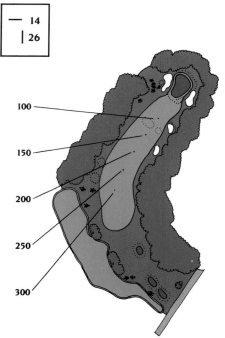

This sixth is not only long, but it also takes a very sharp dogleg to the right. Bunkers nearer the green will penalize those who try to cut the right side.

Hit the drive down the right middle, hopefully, past the corner. The second shot should follow down the left side, opening up the angle to the green.

The small elevated green is sided by two large and deep bunkers. If you find the sand, a blast out to the hole will be necessary to save par.

This seventh is a good short par 4. A drive down the left side is desirable to keep out of the bunker on the right. A second shot is not too long. However, it pays to be short instead of long, since the ground drops off beyond the green, into the trees. An accurate approach will keep the ball to the center of the green and allow for an easy par.

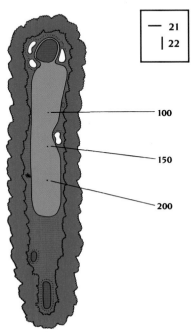

— 21
| 22

100

150

200

ROBBER'S ROW COURSE

8

	BLUE	WHITE	RED
YDS:	165	146	132
PAR:	3	3	3
HDCP:	17	17	17

— 16
| 31

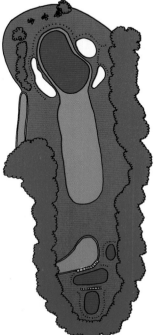

A medium-length par three, requiring a strong shot to the green. The large putting surface slopes to the right. Aim the ball to the right side of the green, bringing it left as necessary. Note the direction and strength of the wind.

A mighty drive down the left side of the fairway will disappear from view as it passes over the ridge just beyond the left bunkers. Water comes in from the left to intimidate you on the approach.

The green is narrow and slopes to the left. A birdie on this hole will turn the front nine with style.

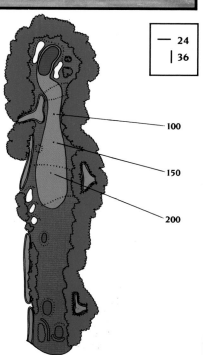

— 24
| 36

100

150

200

10

	BLUE	WHITE	RED
YDS:	471	446	388
PAR:	5	5	5
HDCP:	18	18	14

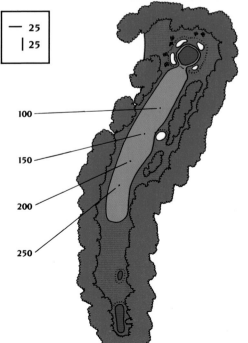

— 25
| 25

100

150

200

250

The tenth starts off the back nine with possibilities. The shortness of the hole allows for the green to be reached in two shots, provided they are two good shots!

A long drive down the right treeline should put the ball in excellent position either to go for the green or lay up. Only one lone bunker is situated on the right side of the fairway — well out of range from the tee.

Bunkers mark the four corners of the green. The elevated surface slopes slowly to the front.

Keeping the ball to the left can be a little bit difficult on this hole. The wind blows left to right, and the fairway slopes down from the left. Fortunately, the approach to the green is best made from the right side.

The drive should be aimed down the left middle of the fairway, allowing the wind and the sloping of the fairway to move the ball right. The second shot should be played to the center of the green, avoiding the three bunkers surrounding it. Be careful not to be long; the water beyond is dangerously close.

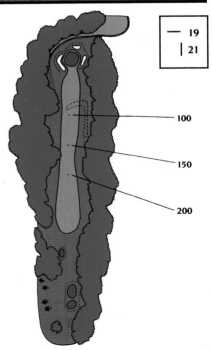

— 19
| 21

100

150

200

ROBBER'S ROW COURSE

12

	BLUE	WHITE	RED
YDS:	164	139	119
PAR:	3	3	3
HDCP:	16	16	18

```
— 26
| 30
```

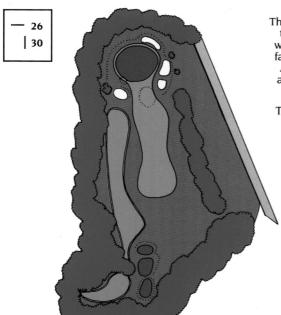

The twelfth is a good par 3. The tee sits in a wide open area, which makes the green appear farther away than it actually is. Add the ingredients of water and bunkers, and the result is a formidable golf hole.

The large green slopes toward the front. Hit the ball to a spot just short of the hole, leaving an uphill putt.

The water sneaks in briefly and then wanders off, only to come back into the picture again near the landing area. The tee is placed back in the trees, so the drive must be hit with care to insure an approach from the fairway.

The green is level with the fairway, with only three bunkers. Accuracy will get the ball close to the flag.

— 23
| 31

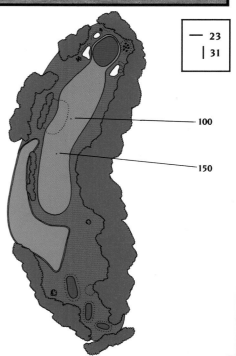

100

150

ROBBER'S ROW COURSE

14

	BLUE	WHITE	RED
YDS:	508	484	421
PAR:	5	5	5
HDCP:	8	8	4

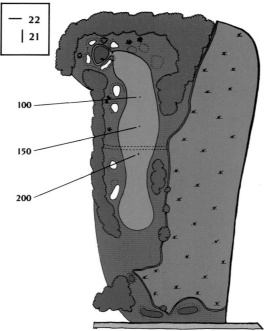

```
— 22
| 21
```

100

150

200

Fortunately, the fairway here goes to the left and not to the right. Otherwise there would be a lot of marshland to cross! Even so, a strong drive is required to maneuver the drive down the middle of the fairway. The second shot must follow down the middle, long enough to get a good view of the putting surface.

Even when just a short distance from this green, the view is less than pleasing. A large bunker sits left front, deterring the hit and run shot up to the flag. A delicately hit approach must stop quickly on the putting surface to avoid going over the green.

This fifteenth can be quite long into the wind. The large putting surface is well visible from the tee because of the mound in the center. The tee shot should be played to the center of the green with enough club to get the ball all the way to the hole.

Unless the ball is right beside the cup, some tricky putts can be expected. The skill of the putter will definitely be put to the test here.

— 23
| 29

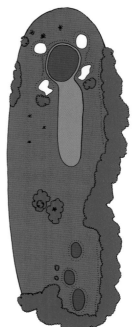

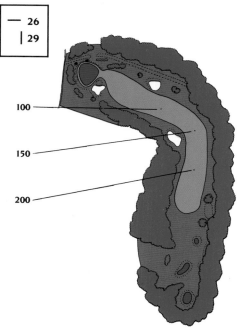

The sixteenth is short, but length is not the factor here. A drive to the right center of the fairway will place the ball in a good angle for the green. A bunker on the inside of the corner will catch those who fall short while trying to cut the corner. Likewise, a bunker past the corner on the right side is waiting to trap corner cutters who go too far!

One large bunker sits ominously to the left front of the green. The putting surface is flat and slightly elevated. Keep the ball from going over the green, for there's water beyond. A par will stretch the match on to the next hole.

The next-to-last is a long par 4, with a dogleg right. The drive must be played long enough to get the ball around the corner, setting up for an easy approach. A fairway bunker on the left implies that the right side is more desirable.

Aim the drive down the right. Expect a medium approach into the green.

The bunkers around the green are deep, so saving par will be an accomplishment. An approach to the heart of the green will make par much simpler.

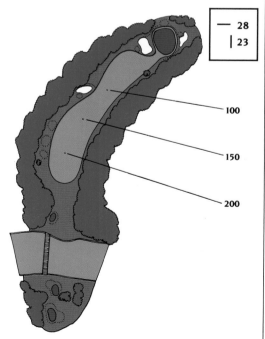

— 28
| 23

100

150

200

18		BLUE	WHITE	RED
	YDS:	491	455	441
	PAR:	5	5	5
	HDCP:	6	6	2

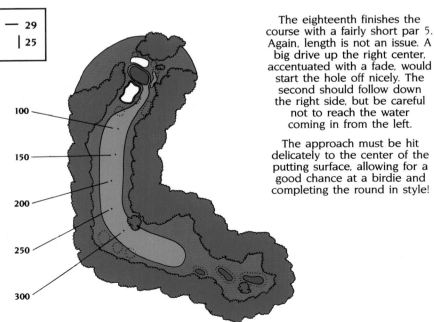

— 29
| 25

100
150
200
250
300

The eighteenth finishes the course with a fairly short par 5. Again, length is not an issue. A big drive up the right center, accentuated with a fade, would start the hole off nicely. The second should follow down the right side, but be careful not to reach the water coming in from the left.

The approach must be hit delicately to the center of the putting surface, allowing for a good chance at a birdie and completing the round in style!

ROBBER'S ROW GOLF COURSE

Port Royal Plantation
P.O. Drawer 7229
Hilton Head Island, SC 29928
803-681-3671
Resort

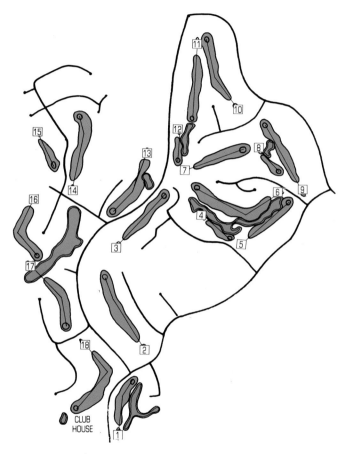

Course	Rating	Slope
Blue	72.1	126
White	69.9	124
Red	70.4	114

Head Professional: Gary S. Duren
Superintendent: David DeGeorge
Designers: George Cobb & Willard Byrd
Teaching Professional: Keith Marks, Sr.

HOLE	1	2	3	4	5	6	7	8	9	OUT	10	11	12	13	14	15	16	17	18	IN	TOTAL
BLUE	317	440	407	199	379	564	367	165	403	3241	471	440	164	404	508	192	375	425	491	3470	6711
WHITE	296	415	364	175	359	527	343	146	368	2993	446	418	139	344	484	169	351	389	455	3195	6188
HDCP	15	3	7	11	9	1	13	17	5		18	2	16	12	8	14	10	4	6		
PAR	4	4	4	3	4	5	4	3	4	35	5	4	3	4	5	3	4	4	5	37	72
RED	264	360	334	148	259	456	276	132	293	2522	388	352	119	314	421	141	307	294	441	2777	5299
HDCP	11	5	3	7	13	1	15	17	9		14	6	18	8	4	16	12	10	2		

The Plantation

The largest and oldest plantation on Hilton Head Island. At over 4500 acres, Sea Pines has enough room for two full-service marinas, miles of oceanside beaches, numerous tennis courts (which include a stadium court), miles of bike paths, a horse stable, and four championship golf courses. The plantation is also home for two major sporting events each year. They are the Family Circle Tennis Tournament and the MCI Heritage Golf Tournament. The golf courses include:

Harbour Town Golf Links

Ocean Golf Course

Sea Marsh Golf Course

Sea Pines Country Club

The Course

This course was designed by Pete Dye with consultation from Jack Nicklaus and opened for play in the fall of 1969 for the inaugural Heritage Golf Classic. Harbour Town Golf Links quickly became world-renowned as a very tough and demanding golf course. The magnificent eighteen hole layout requires the best from the golfer, attracting the top players of the PGA Tour each spring for the MCI Heritage Classic. Truly a shotmaker's golf course, requirng accurate tee shots followed by approaches to 'postage, stamp,' size greens.

The front nine begins with a tight par 4 that plays to a small putting surface. You will quickly recognize the challenge of the course. The distinct collection of par 3's, representative of Pete Dye's unique style, begins with the fourth hole. The eighth is appropriately handicapped as the most difficult hole on the course. The ninth is short, yet includes a U-shaped green which is fronted by a large bunker and backed by a deep pot bunker. The front is only the beginning; the back nine is where it starts to get tough!

The tenth, eleventh, and twelfth start the second nine with long fairways to small, well, protected greens. The thirteenth is an exceptional par 4 requiring excellent position. The fourteenth is a beautiful par 3 that can make or break the round. The fifteenth is considered one of the toughest par 5's in the country. The sixteenth, seventeenth and eighteenth are the most televised holes on the course during the tournament. Yet their beauty is overshadowed by their difficulty. There's not a better sight on the island than the one found on the way up the eighteenth at the end of the day.

Stepping onto this first tee, you are reminded that this is the home of the MCI Heritage Classic. Your nerves may tighten as you take a look down the long narrow fairway. But stay cool, and remember you're here for the enjoyment. Leave the tension to the pros.

Aim the drive down the right center of the fairway for good positioning. Any tee shots left will have to contend with the large trees blocking most shots. Play the second shot to the center of the green. (Even though it is small it still has a center.) Remember, Harbour Town Golf Links requires accuracy. Play conservatively.

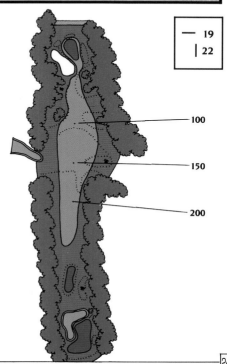

— 19
| 22

100

150

200

HARBOUR TOWN GOLF LINKS

2

	HERITAGE	MEN	LADIES
YDS:	505	481	420
PAR:	5	5	5
HDCP:	9	9	3

The waste bunkers found on this hole as well as a few others are treated differently than sand bunkers. Grounding the club and taking practice swings is allowed.

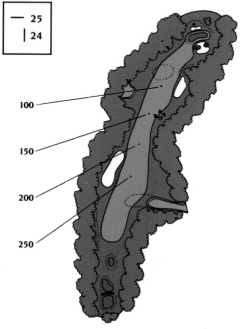

— 25
| 24

100

150

200

250

This fairway is a bit wider than the first hole, but don't be misled. A well-hit drive is still required, especially into the wind. The first hole may not have been as well played as you had planned — so let it go. This second hole can get you back into the game. Play the drive down the left center of the fairway, being careful to stay out of the waste bunker on the left. The second shot should also be played down the left side of the fairway in order to open up the green. Hit the approach shot close to the pin, sink the putt and you're back in business!

HARBOUR TOWN GOLF LINKS

	HERITAGE	MEN	LADIES
YDS:	411	342	297
PAR:	4	4	4
HDCP:	15	15	11

3

From the tee it seems as though playing down the left side is the way to go on this hole. However, the trees to the left actually come out a bit farther than they seem to be. Play down the right side for a good angle on the approach. A large bunker is short right. Four other bunkers are found spread around to the right. Play the second shot to the heart of the green. A 4 is a good score on this hole. The next may be a little more intimidating.

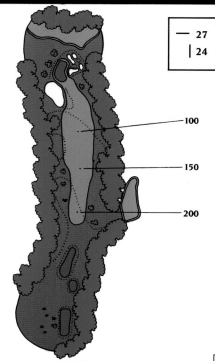

— 27
| 24

100

150

200

HARBOUR TOWN GOLF LINKS

4

	HERITAGE	MEN	LADIES
YDS:	198	160	131
PAR:	3	3	3
HDCP:	11	11	17

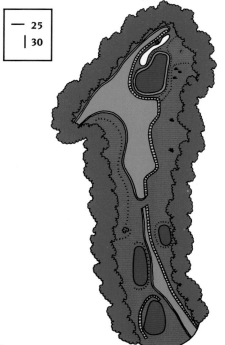

— 25
| 30

Almost an island green, but not quite. Obviously, any shot left of the green will find the water. With the water short left and a bunker beyond, the shot off the tee should be played safely to the right side.

When the pin is placed on the left side, it is advisable to play for the center of the green instead of taking a risky shot.

Be aware of the strong winds above the tree-line.

HARBOUR TOWN GOLF LINKS

	HERITAGE	MEN	LADIES	
YDS:	535	515	432	**5**
PAR:	5	5	5	
HDCP:	3	3	1	

This par 5 can be long into the wind. However, when played well, it can give up a birdie or two. A dogleg to the left, this hole is best played with a tee shot down the middle. Fairway bunkers left and right will be avoided and a good position for the second shot will be found. Play the second down the left side. The hole will encourage a shot down the right. However, a large bunker and tree to the right will spoil any clear approaches to the green. The approach is made to a narrow green that slopes viciously to the right. Play for the left side to let the ball roll down to the flag. Be careful of the bunkers to the left.

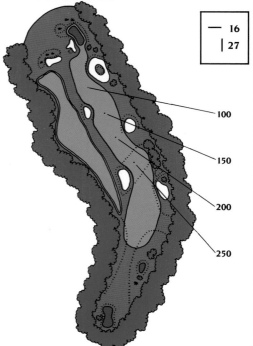

```
—  16
|  27
```

100

150

200

250

245

HARBOUR TOWN GOLF LINKS

6

	HERITAGE	MEN	LADIES
YDS:	419	379	304
PAR:	4	4	4
HDCP:	5	5	13

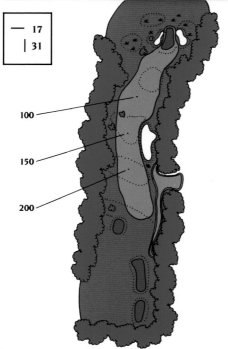

The elevated tee will instill the urge to hit a big drive off this tee. A waste bunker makes its presence known halfway down the right side. The trees along the left slowly move into play. Keep the ball down the right middle of the fairway. The approach is to a long narrow green bordered by bunkers left and right. Note that the area around the green opens up, so a wind not felt from the fairway may surprise you toward the green.

At one time the trees were closing in on this green. A clear shot to the putting surface was a near impossibility! Now that the trees have been cut back, the green is more visible. Water transits the hole from right to left, but this is not the main concern. The sand around the green is another story. It almost completely surrounds this overly undulated putting surface. Get it close. Any putts outside of 15 feet can result in a three-putt adventure!

— 17
| 31

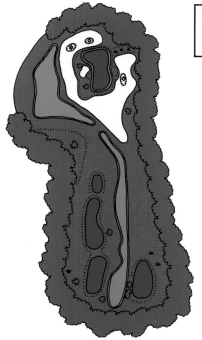

HARBOUR TOWN GOLF LINKS

8

	HERITAGE	MEN	LADIES
YDS:	462	422	353
PAR:	4	4	4
HDCP:	1	1	5

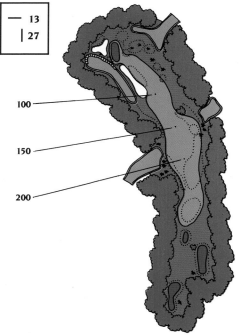

— 13
| 27

100

150

200

From this angle the large oak stands out as a formidable obstacle to be avoided. The small green slopes right, away from the bunkers and water to the left. The tee shot should be played directly for the large oak. A long drive, however, may be blocked out by this tree if the ball wanders off to the right. Ranked as the most difficult hole on the golf course, this long eighth will surely earn your respect.

Not a very long hole, but challenging nonetheless. The U-shaped green is hidden among the pines. Any shot left or right off the tee can, and probably will be, blocked out from the trees. Back off a bit on the drive and play for position. A check with the yardage will indicate that distance is not needed on this hole. Here is where you will learn that Harbour Town is definitely a shotmaker's golf course.

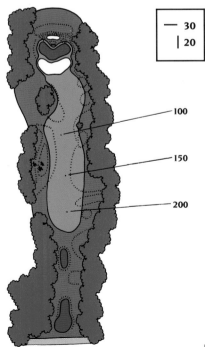

— 30
| 20

100

150

200

HARBOUR TOWN GOLF LINKS

10

	HERITAGE	MEN	LADIES
YDS:	436	352	326
PAR:	4	4	4
HDCP:	10	10	6

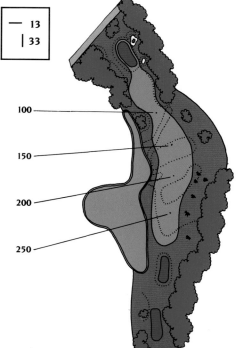

— 13
| 33

100
150
200
250

Turning the corner at Harbour Town, you'll find, is very demanding. The tenth, eleventh and twelfth combine both length and narrow fairways to create a trio of though holes. This tenth starts off at a mere 418 yards from all the way back. A slight dogleg left with water along the left side, this par 4 has an open driving area but a green that is tucked in among the trees.

A strong drive down the middle (probably into the wind) will leave a long approach into the green. The long, narrow green has one small bunker front right, followed by a grass bunker, and then a large bunker back right. Keep the ball on line to the hole. The small flat green is susceptible to one-putts.

The eleventh must be played out of a chute off the tee. The fairway opens up at the landing area. However, do not allow the drive to stray left or right. Water hazards sneak in from both sides. Keep the drive in the center to allow for a good approach to the green.

The putting surface is wedged between bunkers. A large oak front right will repel the shot coming in from the right. Play the fade or straight to the left side. The surface can be slippery, so be careful on the putts.

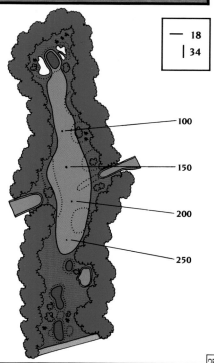

— 18
| 34

100

150

200

250

	HERITAGE	MEN	LADIES
YDS:	413	383	290
PAR:	4	4	4
HDCP:	8	8	14

— 24
| 37

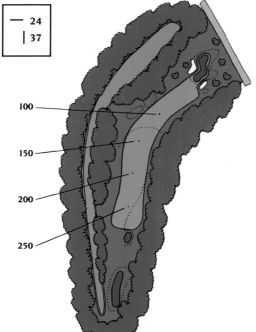

100

150

200

250

The treeline along the right side will most likely block any shot to the green if the drive is not kept to the left. The S-shaped green can preside over some tricky pin placements.

Drive the ball down the left side. A long approach shot can be expected. A pin located on the right can relinquish a birdie; a pin placed on the left can mean a bogey, or more. The large bunker short and left will make the green beyond very short. But with enough club and a smooth stroke, this hole can be conquered!

HARBOUR TOWN GOLF LINKS

	HERITAGE	MEN	LADIES	
YDS:	378	335	302	**13**
PAR:	4	4	4	
HDCP:	12	12	4	

When first described to me, I had envisioned this hole with a bunker surrounding the green that required a ten foot latter to get to it — fortunately that was only my imagination!

This thirteenth helps prove the theory that a good golf hole does not have to be long to be difficult. Accurate shot making is a must on this hole. The drive, as well as the approach, must be hit very well in order to get a par. The island-style green is Dye's original. The boards surrounding the green can deflect a seemingly well-hit sand shot. Play the approach for the center of the green. Avoiding the bunker is a must!

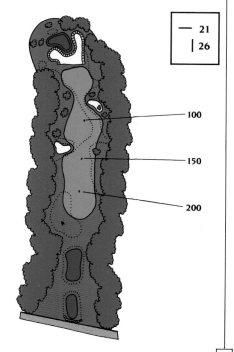

— 21
| 26

100

150

200

HARBOUR TOWN GOLF LINKS

14

	HERITAGE	MEN	LADIES
YDS:	165	138	97
PAR:	3	3	3
HDCP:	18	18	16

The back left bunker looks as though it was created by a grenade, deep and impossible. A unique characteristic that was true of the old courses.

— 19
| 33

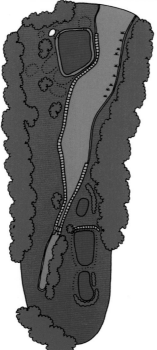

Simply the most beautiful hole during tournament time! With flowers in full bloom, it is difficult to remember the task at hand. Not a long par 3, but relentless just the same, this fourteenth can make or break a round. This is not the time to be concerned whether you brought enough golf balls. Simply get the ball over the water and onto the putting surface. The large, undulating green is now much larger than it originally was. Three putts are possible, but easily avoided if care is taken on the first putt. Pars will be respectable.

Described as the best par 5 in golf, this fifteenth will gain your respect. A narrow path lined with trees will allow no leeway on the drive. The fairway does not open up at the landing area, so accuracy is a must off the tee. The second shot will open up a bit off to the right. Play the second down the right side to avoid the water hazard left. Such a long hole may call for a long iron for the approach. The new larger green is receptive to well hit shots. Note the putting surface has two tiers, left and right. An accurate shot to the flag may yield birdies, but a shot to the wrong side of the green may yield a bogey. Go for broke!

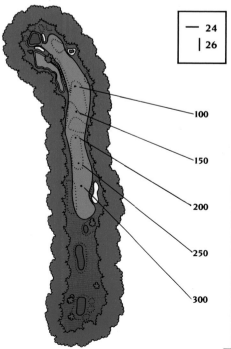

— 24
| 26

100

150

200

250

300

HARBOUR TOWN GOLF LINKS

16

	HERITAGE	MEN	LADIES
YDS:	376	316	240
PAR:	4	4	4
HDCP:	16	16	12

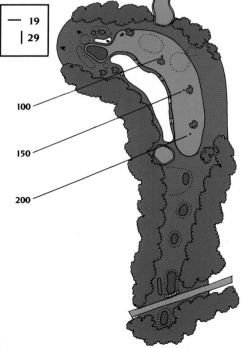

— 19

| 29

100

150

200

The sixteenth illustrates a different concept. The large waste bunker, which runs the entire length of the fairway, may entice a few to play within. The hole itself, bends to the left. A sharp turn to the left brings the ocean into view. Winds around the corner can be take you by surprise. Play accordingly. Whether the approach is made from the waste bunker or the fairway, be advised that this green can be tricky. The surface slopes from back to front. Be careful not to hit the shot past the hole. A slippery downhill putt will be the consequence.

This hole can play short or very, very long. Downwind the 192-yard Heritage tees can play around twenty yards shorter. However, into the gusting wind, the hole can easily seem thirty yards longer! Note the wind direction. With the right club, the shot should be played to the right side of the green. A pin placement to the back left corner will draw a few shots toward the water. Play this hole strong. Championships have been won on it!

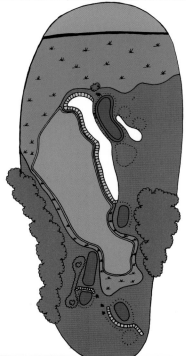

— 22
| 33

	HERITAGE	MEN	LADIES
YDS:	478	458	330
PAR:	4	4	4
HDCP:	2	2	8

— 17
| 28

100
150
200
250

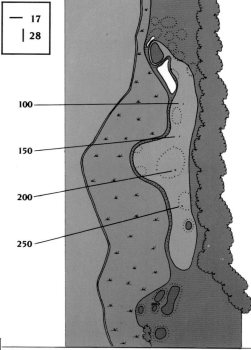

The lighthouse. Maybe the biggest attention-getter on the island. It is, however, a good reference point for aiming the drive on this mighty eighteenth. A strong drive down the right middle of the fairway will keep the ball away from the ocean. Be careful, though. Out-of-bounds is to the right. A long approach can be expected. Play smart, the ocean is now in play!

A par on this hole is an achievement of note. A birdie ranks you with the champions!

HARBOUR TOWN GOLF LINKS

Sea Pines Plantation
11 Lighthouse Lane
Hilton Head Island, SC 29928
803-671-2446
Resort

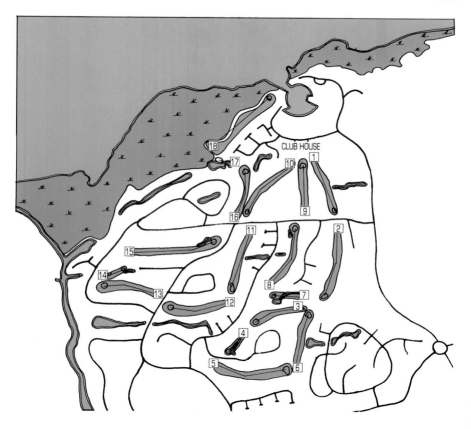

Director of Golf: Cary Corbitt
Head Professional: Greg MacDonell
Superintendent: Gary Wilder
Architects: Pete Dye & Jack Nicklaus
Teaching Professional: Don Trahan

Course	Rating	Slope
Heritage	74.0	134
Men	70.0	125
Ladies	69.0	117

HOLE	1	2	3	4	5	6	7	8	9	OUT	10	11	12	13	14	15	16	17	18	IN	TOTAL
BLUE	414	505	411	198	535	419	180	462	337	3461	436	438	413	378	165	575	376	192	478	3451	6912
WHITE	328	481	342	160	515	379	140	422	310	3077	352	392	383	335	138	507	316	161	458	3042	6119
HDCP	13	9	15	11	3	5	17	1	7		10	4	8	12	18	6	16	14	2		
PAR	4	5	4	3	5	4	3	4	4	36	4	4	4	4	3	5	4	3	4	35	71
RED	300	420	297	131	432	304	94	353	275	2606	326	314	290	302	97	417	240	97	330	2413	5019
HDCP	7	3	11	17	1	13	15	5	9		6	10	14	4	16	2	12	18	8		

The Course

Designed by George Cobb and opened for play in 1962, this was the first Hilton Head Island golf course, as well as the first for Sea Pines Plantation , where original plans called for a single eighteen-hole golf course. This course was to provide spectacular golf with the scenery to match, and it has not disappointed. It is located in the heart of the plantation, adorned with beautiful oaks and sea pines throughout. A breathtaking view is to be had from the green of the fifteenth, where the course has ventured out toward the ocean. All of this beauty notwithstanding, players will quickly realize the challenge that the Ocean Golf Course has to offer.

The front nine starts off with a fairly easy par 4. Yet, at only 327 yards, this first hole can get the adrenaline pumping early, a good thing, because it will be needed on the next few holes! The second can be the most difficult on the course. At 439 yards, it's a quick turnaround from the short first hole. If the first few holes can be completed without high numbers, then the rest of the day should prove to be successful.

Around the turn to the backside is another easy-starting hole. The designer has provided the opportunities; it's up to the player to take advantage of them! Birdies are possible for the first half of this back nine. Par will be an achievement on the finishing holes, where length and accuracy are big requirements.

Upon completion, most will agree that the Ocean Golf Course is as tough as any course around — with spectacular views to match!

OCEAN GOLF COURSE

	BLUE	WHITE	RED
YDS:	327	311	289
PAR:	4	4	4
HDCP:	13	13	9

1

The Ocean Course is one of George Cobb's more difficult golf courses. He designed the course with relatively easy holes starting the nines, then added length and substance to finish the nines. For a satisfying total score, you have to have a strong finish.

This first hole, not overly long, is a good warmup hole. A slight dogleg leaves the green in view. Some of the really long hitters may even think the green is drivable — with a cannon! The elevated tee sets the stage. A strong drive down the middle will leave a short approach into the right sloping green. The bunker in front is not large, but the lip is big, giving the impression of size. Leaving the approach short of the hole is advisable in order to have an uphill putt.

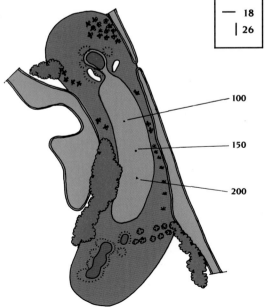

— 18
| 26

100

150

200

OCEAN GOLF COURSE

2

	BLUE	WHITE	RED
YDS:	439	382	351
PAR:	4	4	4
HDCP:	1	1	1

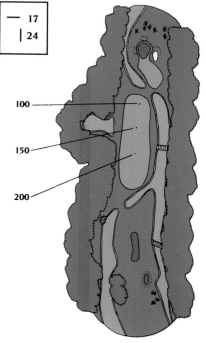

— 17
| 24

100

150

200

The second hole is an indication of the length that can be found on this course. Usually into the wind, this par 4 should make you wary of what is yet to come. Two solid golf shots are needed to get the ball on the dance floor. The water along the right side is both intimidating and hungry. Some do not realize the amount of room there actually is to the left, and they wind up wet. Play the drive down the left side. A decision may have to be made on the second: Lay up or go for it. The elevated green is small and flat. Once on, most putts are not too long. The trick is to get on there!

OCEAN GOLF COURSE

	BLUE	WHITE	RED
YDS:	173	149	115
PAR:	3	3	3
HDCP:	15	15	17

3

Also, into the wind, this hole can be long. Care should be taken that enough club is being used. Palms line the left side, and water covers the front and right. A well hit shot should be played to the flagstick. Note the large size of the putting surface. A pin placed to the right rear of the green can make the hole difficult to get to.

— 20
| 35

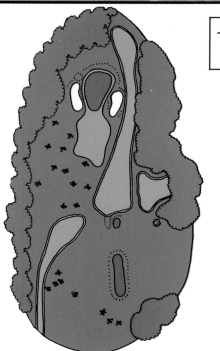

OCEAN GOLF COURSE

4

	BLUE	WHITE	RED
YDS:	484	471	424
PAR:	5	5	5
HDCP:	11	11	3

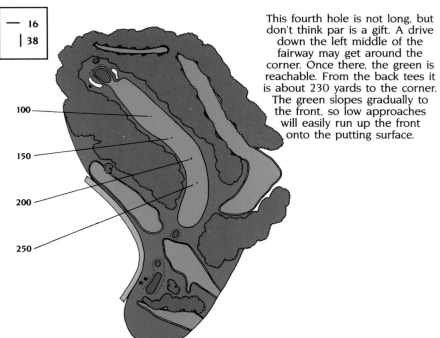

— 16
| 38

100
150
200
250

This fourth hole is not long, but don't think par is a gift. A drive down the left middle of the fairway may get around the corner. Once there, the green is reachable. From the back tees it is about 230 yards to the corner. The green slopes gradually to the front, so low approaches will easily run up the front onto the putting surface.

On first glimpse, one would be tempted to hit the drive down the right side. Wrong! Although this hole is short and the distance can be greatly reduced if a route is taken straight-on to the hole, it is safer and simpler to play down the middle or left side. This way the green is opened up for an easy approach. The putting surface slopes gently toward the front, making the cup easily visible. Simply put a good move on the ball and watch it bounce up to the hole.

— 26
| 32

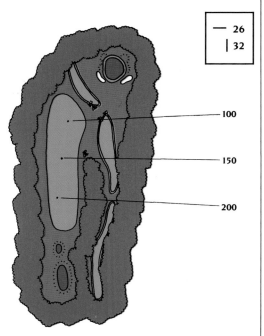

100

150

200

		BLUE	WHITE	RED
6	YDS:	408	394	324
	PAR:	4	4	4
	HDCP:	3	3	7

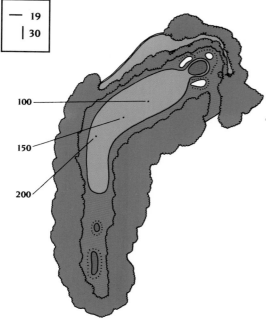

— 19
| 30

100

150

200

The sixth cuts viciously to the right. A strong drive down the middle to the right side is needed to get the ball in position for the approach. This hole always plays longer than it looks. Use one more club and play for the center of the green. Bunkers left and right are best avoided. Expect a slippery downhill putt if the ball rolls left past the hole.

Length is the biggest issue here. The wind makes it seem as if the treeline is closing in on you. Accuracy is key. The bunker left front looms ominously on the horizon. The putting surface slopes drastically to the right. A par 3 is to be proud. And bogeys aren't bad on this one!

— 25
| 34

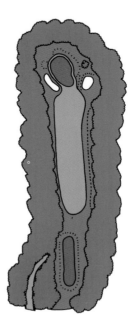

—	19
|	27

100

150

200

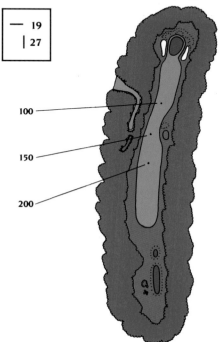

This eighth looks straight-away. However, the fairway moves curiously to the left. Mr. Cobb has widened the fairway on purpose. In fact, to get the play down the left side he has placed a fairway bunker just within reach to the right. Better go as designed and play down the left side. The approach is made to another forward sloping green. By now your putter should be used to this scenario!

The ninth is a good finishing hole. A birdie can be achieved if it's needed. The fairway zigs and zags toward the hole. Aim the drive down the right side. The second should come back to the left, followed by a short approach to the large green.
The bunker, front right, creates an illusion that the green is closer than it is. Pay attention to the yardage marked off on the course.

Knock the approach close and putt the ball into the cup for the bird. A strong finish!

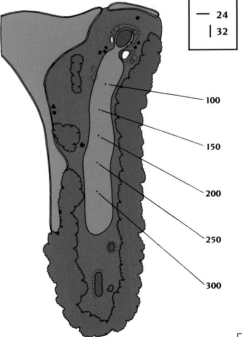

— 24
| 32

100

150

200

250

300

OCEAN GOLF COURSE

10

	BLUE	WHITE	RED
YDS:	370	349	256
PAR:	4	4	4
HDCP:	12	12	14

— 18
| 32

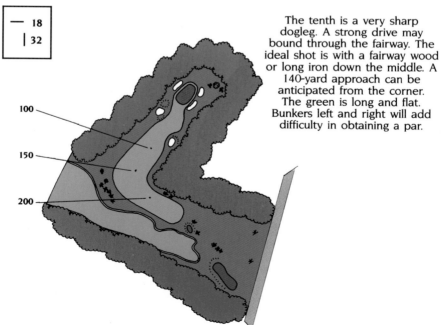

100

150

200

The tenth is a very sharp dogleg. A strong drive may bound through the fairway. The ideal shot is with a fairway wood or long iron down the middle. A 140-yard approach can be anticipated from the corner. The green is long and flat. Bunkers left and right will add difficulty in obtaining a par.

OCEAN GOLF COURSE

	BLUE	WHITE	RED	**11**
YDS:	169	154	136	
PAR:	3	3	3	
HDCP:	18	18	18	

This par 3, although straight with no water, can be a difficult hole. The wind picks up above the treeline. A seemingly well hit shot will be pushed back by the wind, falling short of the green. The treeline to the right may also grab a few balls that wander too close. Play down to the left center of the green. Once on the putting surface, the putts should drop quite easily.

— 23
| 24

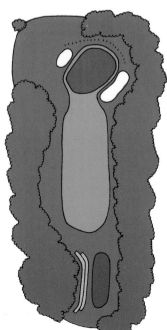

OCEAN GOLF COURSE

12

	BLUE	WHITE	RED
YDS:	378	351	282
PAR:	4	4	4
HDCP:	14	14	12

— 28
| 31

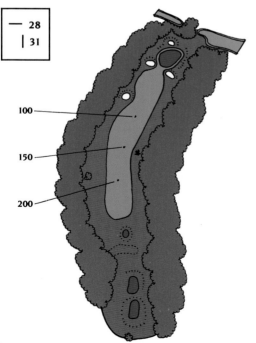

100
150
200

The fairway opens up to the left. Playing down the right side may leave an approach that's blocked out by the trees. Play down the middle. A drive left will be in the fairway, but will increase yardage to the approach. Fairly flat on the back, the putting surface slopes rapidly to the front. Slippery putts can be expected when the pin is situated up front.

	BLUE	WHITE	RED
YDS:	355	332	305
PAR:	4	4	4
HDCP:	8	8	2

13

A pond looms ominously in the foreground of the green. A long drive up the right may roll into the water. Play down the left side, getting the ball in position for the approach. The green angles up to the right. A solid shot to the flag is needed to keep the ball dry and on the putting surface. Shots just short may end up wet.

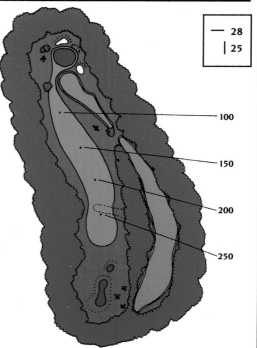

— 28
| 25

100

150

200

250

	BLUE	WHITE	RED
YDS:	475	461	416
PAR:	5	5	5
HDCP:	16	16	8

14

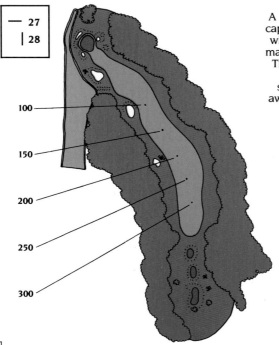

— 27

| 28

100

150

200

250

300

A short par 5, this fourteenth is capable of lifting spirits. With the wind at the back, longer hitters may be able to get home in two. The rest of us must play down the middle with three solid shots, placing the ball inches away from the cup on the third.

Ocean's most breathtaking hole. The view from the tee looks is like a vision of the wild blue yonder. The beating of the waves on the beach instill a sense of awe. A big shot is going to be needed to get this ball to the green.

The back tees are a mere 207 yards, but the onshore breeze from the ocean might as well increase it by another 20 to 30 yards. Play strong, but be careful not to let the ball go left or right. Out-of-bounds is to the right, and a mess of trees is to the left.

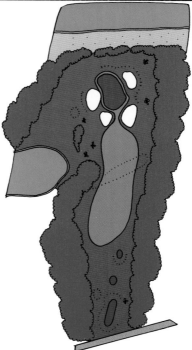

— 24
| 34

OCEAN GOLF COURSE

16

	BLUE	WHITE	RED
YDS:	449	423	323
PAR:	4	4	4
HDCP:	2	2	6

— 22
| 23

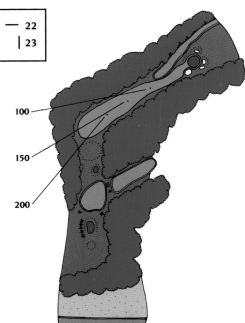

100

150

200

These three finishing holes can be the most demanding on the island. This sixteeth takes a sharp dogleg right. With the strong winds off the ocean at the back, a good drive is simple. A long drive down the left middle may bound through the fairway. Keep the ball in the middle or a little right. A long approach can be expected into the green, which is amply protected by water left and bunkers right. The right front bunker creates a deceptive image that the green is closer. Do not be tricked. One club more than usual is a must.

OCEAN GOLF COURSE

	BLUE	WHITE	RED
YDS:	536	523	426
PAR:	5	5	5
HDCP:	4	4	4

17

The length, the water and the wind make this seventeenth a true test of golfing ability. The tee shot should be played down the left; there's a lot more room than it looks like. The second shot may call for a decision: Lay up or go for it. The "lay-up" should be played again down the left side, leaving a long approach to the green. In contrast, the "go" must be played to the right middle.

A large, flat putting surface is the target. The approach shot that is played to the flagstick will be easily knocked into the hole. Competition will weaken with a birdie on this hole.

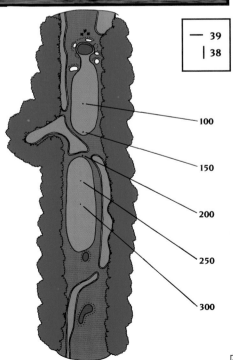

— 39
| 38

100

150

200

250

300

OCEAN GOLF COURSE

18

	BLUE	WHITE	RED
YDS:	408	363	313
PAR:	4	4	4
HDCP:	6	6	10

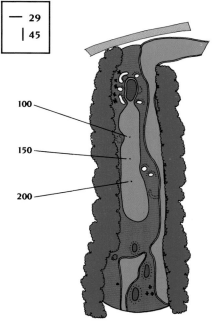

— 29
| 45

100

150

200

The last two holes may have been tiring, and the eighteenth doesn't let up. A strong drive down the middle is necessary in order for the green to be reachable. Fairway bunkers right help you to decide on a drive to the left.

The approach is to another very large green. Note the location of the flagstick. As many as two more clubs may be needed. Upon sinking the last putt, take a breather. These last few holes were tough!

OCEAN GOLF COURSE

Sea Pines Plantation
100 North Sea Pines Drive
Hilton Head Island, SC 29928
803-671-2446
Public

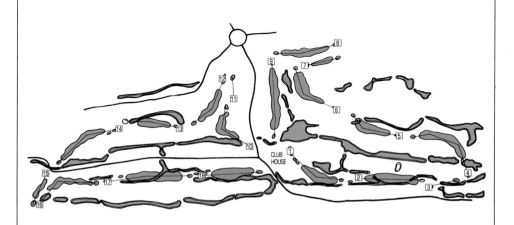

Director of Golf: Cary Corbitt
Head Professional: John F. Farrell
Superintendent: Ricky Wideman
Designer: George Cobb
Teaching Professional: Rick Barry

Course	Rating	Slope
Blue	71.0	125
White	70.0	119
Red	70.0	111

HOLE	1	2	3	4	5	6	7	8	9	OUT	10	11	12	13	14	15	16	17	18	IN	TOTAL
BLUE	327	439	173	484	330	408	216	395	495	3267	370	169	378	355	475	207	449	536	408	3347	6213
WHITE	311	382	149	471	309	394	201	372	478	3067	349	154	351	332	461	190	423	523	363	3146	6213
HDCP	13	1	15	11	17	3	5	7	9		12	18	14	8	16	10	2	4	6		
PAR	4	4	3	5	4	4	3	4	5	36	4	3	4	4	5	3	4	5	4	36	72
RED	289	351	115	424	266	324	179	329	423	2700	256	136	282	305	416	127	323	426	313	2584	5284
HDCP	9	1	17	3	13	7	11	15	5		14	18	12	2	8	16	6	4	10		

SEA MARSH
GOLF COURSE

The Course

Sea Marsh golf course was designed by George Cobb. In 1964, the course con-
sisted of only nine holes, called the Live Oak Nine. These nine holes were eventually
increased to a total of eighteen, establishing the course as the Sea Marsh golf
course. Completed and open for play in 1967, the course was the third one of the
very first few built on Hilton Head Island. Located at the Plantation Club in Sea
Pines, this is a fun layout. With the improvements made in the summer of 1990,
under the direction of Clyde Johnston, the course has been made what it was
originally designed to be — a golf course that provides beauty among the Spanish
Moss-draped trees while offering a demanding test of the golfer's ability.

Although the front nine is not too long at 3200 yards, its shortness is not to be
discounted. Sharp doglegs, strategically placed fairway bunkers, and large undulating greens require the best from the golfer. The first tee beckons a mighty drive
to an open landing area that just happens to be on the far side of a large pond. It
takes accurate driving to keep the fairways under control, and smart putting to con-
quer the large greens.

Not having returned to the clubhouse after the ninth hole, the course turns back
on the tenth. An easy par 4 starts off the second nine with an opportunity for birdie. Take advantage of it; birdies do not come easily on this side. Except for the fourteenth and eighteenth holes, the back nine features lengthy fairways that are usually
into the wind.

SEA MARSH GOLF COURSE

	BLUE	WHITE	RED
YDS:	366	325	230
PAR:	4	4	4
HDCP:	15	15	17

Stepping up to this tee takes true grit, as you'll soon find out. Play the drive down the left side of the fairway, keeping well clear of the fairway bunkers and getting the ball over the water in a hurry. From the drive, the approach is easy. The green is elevated and protected by bunkers front right and right.

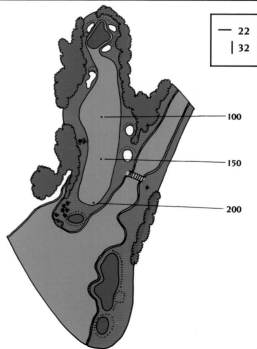

— 22
| 32

— 100

— 150

— 200

SEA MARSH GOLF COURSE

2

	BLUE	WHITE	RED
YDS:	301	280	271
PAR:	4	4	4
HDCP:	13	13	13

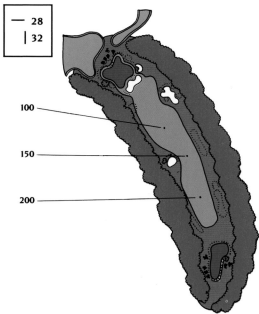

— 28

| 32

100

150

200

The hole may look short, but do not underestimate it. Trees along the left side are notorious for grabbing a well-hit drive. Stay clear, and play a short drive down the right side. Even playing conservatively, you can come in sub-par on this hole. A large elevated green has replaced the old small green. Elevated and surrounded by bunkers, this new green is a welcome change.

Wide and straight, this hole may catch you off guard if you're not careful. It may look simple enough, but, a drive down the center is necessary to avoid the fairway bunkers left and right. The approach is made to a large front sloping green. Go for the flag. Birdies are possible.

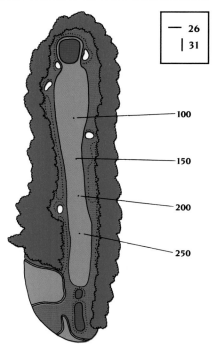

— 26
| 31

100

150

200

250

	BLUE	WHITE	RED
YDS:	200	185	127
PAR:	3	3	3
HDCP:	11	11	11

Always aim for the center of the green—unless the pin is in the center, then aim for the edges.
—Anonymous

— 16
| 33

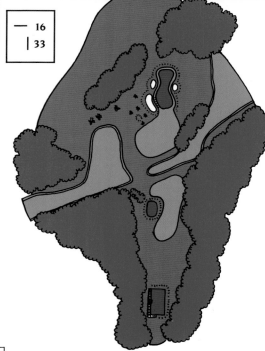

You may have tightened the reins on the last hole, so keep it up on this hole. Water, trees right, and bunkers left and right may be intimidating. Ignore them. Out of sight, out of mind! Focus on the putting surface. Keeping the ball short of the hole may be advised in order to have an uphill putt and avoid the slope beyond the green.

The green is not visible from the tee box. Although you may be inclined to drive down the right side to cut the corner of this dogleg, back off and play the ball down the right center. The approach shot can be longer than it looks. Be sure to use enough club.

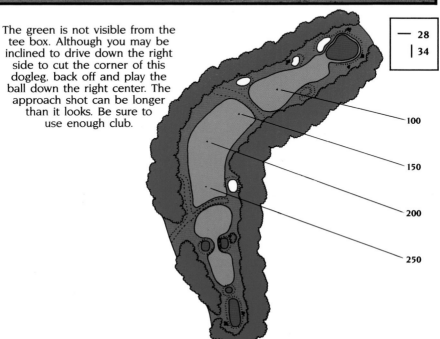

— 28
| 34

100

150

200

250

SEA MARSH GOLF COURSE

6

	BLUE	WHITE	RED
YDS:	478	463	409
PAR:	5	5	5
HDCP:	9	9	9

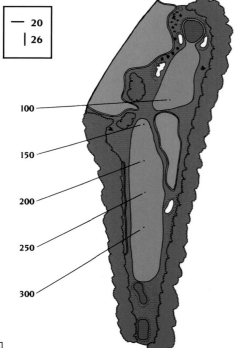

The sixth hole is a fairly short par 5, but beware of "water, water everywhere"! The green can be reached in two, although longer hitters may want to back off a little with the driver. A large pond looms within the tee shot landing area. Play the drive down the left side. Whether going for the green in two or not, the left side is the best side to avoid the water. Water creeps in from the left near the green. The second shot should be more to the right. The elevated putting surface has two bunkers, left and right. Putts can be made on the flat surface.

SEA MARSH GOLF COURSE

	BLUE	WHITE	RED
YDS:	162	140	105
PAR:	3	3	3
HDCP:	17	17	15

This short par 3 can look simple enough, but don't be fooled. The three bunkers surrounding the green will grab any stray shots off the tee. The large putting surface demands accuracy to the flagstick in order to get the putt down in one. Be careful not to hit too long. A small lagoon is just beyond the green.

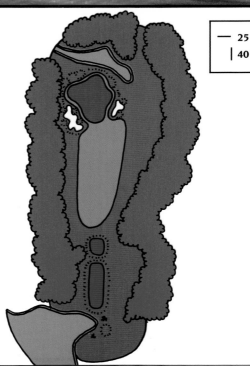

— 25
| 40

SEA MARSH GOLF COURSE

8

	BLUE	WHITE	RED
YDS:	428	403	336
PAR:	4	4	4
HDCP:	1	1	3

— 23
| 27

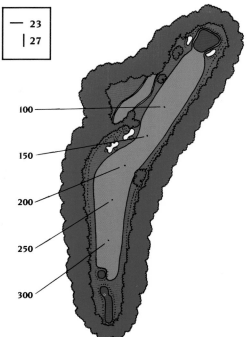

100

150

200

250

300

The eighth can prove to be a bit difficult. Although the urge may be to cut the corner, there is no real advantage to doing so. In fact, the trees come out more than you think. Play the drive for the bunkers located on the left side of the fairway. The angle to the green is much better. Be careful not to hit the ball too far off the tee; the large oak just past the fairway bunkers will get into the act. The putting surface is flat on the back and slopes down toward the front. One bunker left of the green is deep. Best to avoid it!

SEA MARSH GOLF COURSE

9

	BLUE	WHITE	RED
YDS:	505	475	409
PAR:	5	5	5
HDCP:	7	7	1

As some of the older players on the tour brag about the trees that they could hit their drives over — the younger players must realize that the trees were much smaller back then!

Years ago, this ninth-hole dogleg could be cut by a substantial amount. Unfortunately, the trees have grown since then, and this hole has gotten its dignity back. The drive off the tee must be played to the left; that is, a long iron or short wood along the tree-line. The almost 90-degree corner should be played to the center so that the second shot will be unobstructed. Be careful, though. An over-ambitious shot around the corner will find the water just beyond.

The second shot is simply hit toward the green; there is a lot of fairway right and left. The approach is to an elevated two-tiered green. Note the location of the flag. It may be necessary to use a club or two more. Played conservatively, this ninth will relinquish a birdie or two.

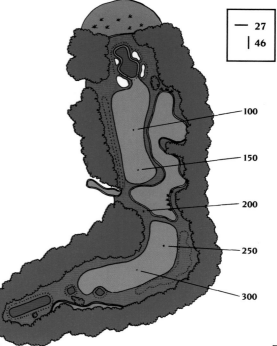

SEA MARSH GOLF COURSE

10

	BLUE	WHITE	RED
YDS:	318	304	270
PAR:	4	4	4
HDCP:	18	18	16

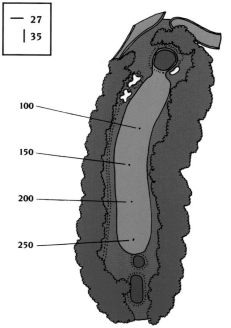

— 27
| 35

100
150
200
250

A fairly short par 4 starts off the back nine. Slight dogleg to the left, this tenth will provide a good birdie opportunity. Two new bunkers down the left side are disconcerting targets from the tee. This picture is from the left of the bunkers—not a good place to be for the second shot.

The approach to the green should be hit clean and crisp. The forward-sloping putting surface will allow the ball to bite and stop. Going for the flag is advised.

The view from the eleventh tee can make this hole look difficult. Water to the left of the tee will give second thoughts about the big drive over the corner. Do not be intimidated. Simply drive the ball just right of the fairway bunker to the left. The length of the hole makes going for the green in two nearly impossible. Plan to play three good shots to the green. Once around the corner, keep the ball down the center. Accuracy is needed on the approach to keep clear of the bunkers surrounding the green. The putting surface has only a hint of undulation. One-putts are possible!

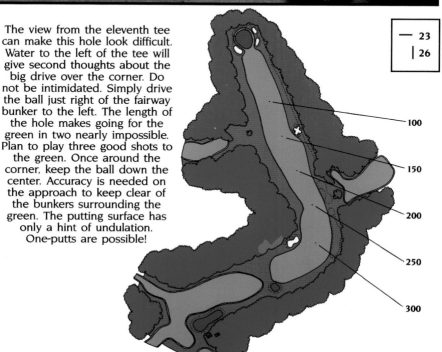

— 23
| 26

100

150

200

250

300

12

	BLUE	WHITE	RED
YDS:	423	410	325
PAR:	4	4	4
HDCP:	4	4	8

— 21
| 26

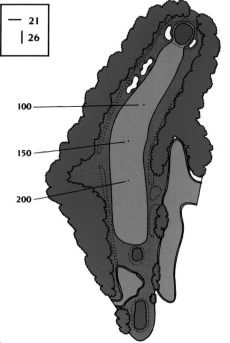

100

150

200

Without the wind this hole is long. With the wind, it can be very long, and unfortunately it is usually into the wind. Play the drive down the middle for the best position. Expect a long approach into the green.

The green is fronted by two bunkers. The elevated surface slopes from back to front. Slippery sidehill putts can be expected. Keep the ball below the hole on the approach — if possible.

	BLUE	WHITE	RED
YDS:	163	151	111
PAR:	3	3	3
HDCP:	10	10	12

Completely reconstructed, this thirteenth is the Sea Marsh signature hole. As beautiful as it is tough, this par 3 will be one to remember. The large undulating green will add dimension to putting. Keep the ball dry and get it on the putting surface. Any shots, of course, can be expected to find either the water or sand.

— 30
| 36

	BLUE	WHITE	RED
YDS:	366	350	310
PAR:	4	4	4
HDCP:	6	6	4

— 22

| 30

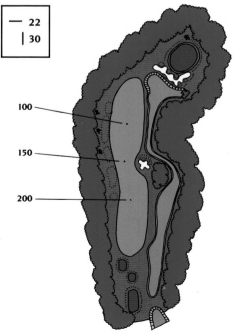

100

150

200

A short par 4 to get back into the game. Although it looks simple enough, play it safe. A drive down the left side will put the ball in excellent position for the approach. New construction around the green makes it similar to the thirteenth.

As on the thirteenth, length is important. Be sure to get the ball to the green to keep it dry. The putting surface slopes diagonally to the front left. An approach left below the flag will leave an uphill putt.

SEA MARSH GOLF COURSE

	BLUE	WHITE	RED
YDS:	411	398	355
PAR:	4	4	4
HDCP:	8	8	2

15

Length is back in the game. The fifteenth bends slightly right. Try to keep the drive down the right middle. The corner is fairly sharp and can be cut just a little. A drive down the left will guarantee tree clearance but may add to the distance.

The approach is to a fairly flat green. Two bunkers, one front left and the second back right, add intimidation to the shot. Par is a score to be proud of on this hole.

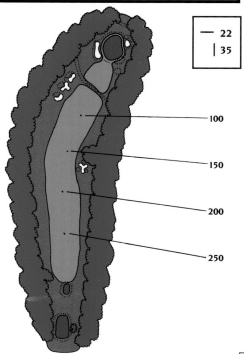

— 22
| 35

100

150

200

250

— 22
| 35

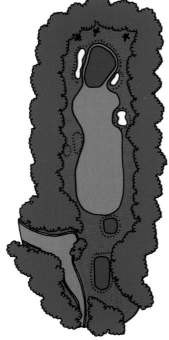

A long par 3 that is usually directly into the wind. A three is needed on this hole to help wrap up the back nine — not to mention closing the door on the competition! A strong shot off the tee is neccessary to get the ball to the flag. Once on the green, the putts should drop. The large, flat putting surface is excellent for rolling the ball right into the hole!

SEA MARSH GOLF COURSE

	BLUE	WHITE	RED
YDS:	504	480	427
PAR:	5	5	5
HDCP:	14	14	10

17

Not too long, but again, this is usually into the wind. With the wind at the back, this hole is reachable in two! Play the drive down the left middle. Playing conservatively, birdies are possible. The second shot should be down the middle; if not, bunkers and water left and right will spoil the third. The elevated putting surface is a good target for the accurate approach shot. Get a birdie, and on to the eighteenth.

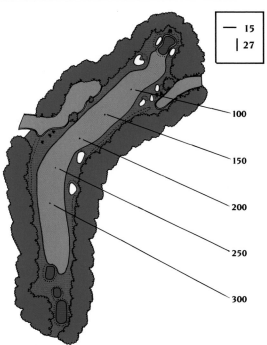

— 15
| 27

100

150

200

250

300

SEA MARSH GOLF COURSE

18

	BLUE	WHITE	RED
YDS:	330	319	268
PAR:	4	4	4
HDCP:	12	12	14

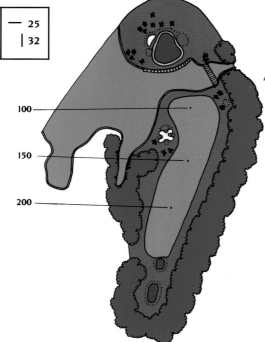

— 25

| 32

100

150

200

The length is definitely not a factor on this last hole. An easy swing with a long iron off the tee leaves an approach just around 140 yards from the flag. A firm second shot to the center of the green will leave a putt of no more than 25 feet from the cup. Two putts a par, one putt and birdie!

SEA MARSH GOLF COURSE

Sea Pines Plantation
Plantation Club
100 North Sea Pines Drive
Hilton Head Island, SC 29928
803-671-2446
Resort

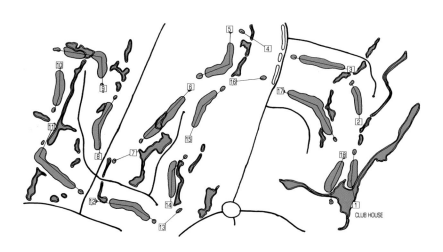

CLUB HOUSE

Director of Golf: Cary Corbitt
Head Professional: John Farrell
Teaching Professional: Rick Barry
Superintendent: Ricky Wideman
Designer: George Cobb

Course	Rating	Slope
Blue	70.0	120
White	69.0	117
Red	69.6	115

HOLE	1	2	3	4	5	6	7	8	9	OUT	10	11	12	13	14	15	16	17	18	IN	TOTAL
BLUE	366	301	381	200	428	478	162	428	505	3249	318	550	423	163	366	411	201	504	330	3266	6515
WHITE	325	280	363	185	412	463	140	403	475	3046	304	530	410	151	350	398	181	480	319	3123	6169
HDCP	15	13	5	11	3	9	17	1	7		18	2	4	10	6	8	16	14	12		
PAR	4	4	4	3	4	5	3	4	5	36	4	5	4	3	4	4	3	5	4	36	72
RED	230	271	320	127	320	409	105	336	409	2527	270	417	325	111	310	355	151	427	268	2634	5161
HDCP	17	13	7	11	5	9	15	3	1		16	6	8	12	4	2	18	10	14		

The Course

This course was designed by Arnold Palmer and opened for play in 1974. Secretly tucked just inside the gates of Sea Pines Plantation, the Sea Pines Country Club golf course surprises all those who play it for the first time. Tight, narrow fairways aptly make up for the shortness of the layout, which is only a little more than 6300 yards. Tall pines line each fairway, making recovery from a strayed shot very difficult. Keeping the ball in the center of the fairway is a must on this course.

From the start, the golfer will realize that the fairway should not be missed. The thick pines have not been thinned out, causing problems for those who haplessly wander from the short grass. While avoiding the trees, be careful to keep an eye out for the water hazards that are constantly present. A conservative approach to this first nine holes will help to get a feel for the course.

The back nine opens with a few rather easy holes, relatively speaking. After the front nine, any hole with a fairway more than 30 yards wide is well appreciated. Approaches are tight, with trees leaning into the greens and blocking out many shots. The finishing holes are not overly long; however, positioning off the tee is imperative. The eighteenth finishes the day with a magnificent view of Calibogue Cay. The round is never that bad when it ends with such a sight.

As you will soon find out, Arnold Palmer has designed an exceptional golf course. The first hole is a good example of what is to come; lots of water bordered by narrow fairways. Although the trees along the right side look as though they can be carried, play the tee shot safely down the left center for a good look at the hole. A drive well placed down the left center will leave the player with a clear approach shot to the green. This approach can also look closer than it actually is — especially into the wind. Be sure to use enough club.

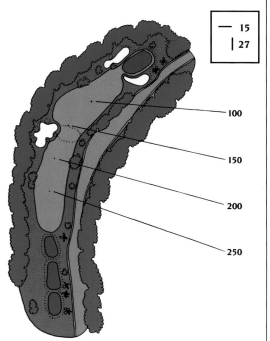

— 15
| 27

100
150
200
250

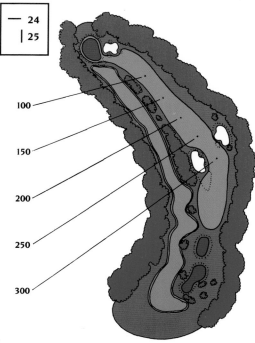

— 24

| 25

100

150

200

250

300

A fairly short par 5 is a breather before the onslaught. With the wind at your back, you may have the urge to give the drive a good bust. Resist it. Fairway bunkers left and right will gladly spoil your day. A more judicious decision will be to play down the middle conservatively. Play for the green in regulation in order to have a short approach shot that can be controlled. The longer hitters may try for this green in two, but that's a risky move considering the well-guarded putting surface. The large bunker right front and water hazard to the left can add a few unplanned strokes to the score.

SEA PINES COUNTRY CLUB

	BLUE	WHITE	RED
YDS:	345	334	318
PAR:	4	4	4
HDCP:	15	15	9

3

This par 4 will boost the ego. Short and fairly wide, this hole is ripe for the birdies! Although a healthy drive snugly down the right side would leave a very short approach, be smart and play down the left center. An iron would probably be the best choice, since the idea is position. The second shot should be from the left center of the fairway into a green sloping toward the fairway. A swell in the middle of the green will give the illusion that the pin is closer than it really is. Pay attention to the yardage.

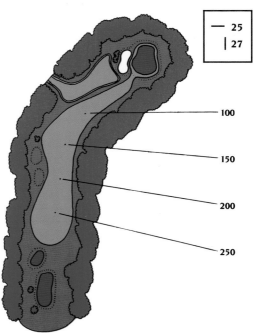

— 25
| 27

100

150

200

250

SEA PINES COUNTRY CLUB

4		BLUE	WHITE	RED
	YDS:	145	135	115
	PAR:	3	3	3
	HDCP:	17	17	17

— 25
| 28

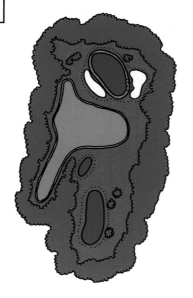

Hidden among the pines, this par 3 will look simple enough. But watch out! The wind above the treeline can play havoc with a well-hit shot. Green slopes toward the tee-box. (Throwing darts comes to mind.) Bunkers left and right distract the attention from the water hazard. Use enough club. It's easy to see the hazards between the tee and the green, but again, be careful not to overshoot the green. A large mound beyond the green will help the long shot farther on its way. Other than those few hazards the hole is straightforward. Simply hit the ball on the green and two-putt for par. . .

SEA PINES COUNTRY CLUB

	BLUE	WHITE	RED
YDS:	532	490	421
PAR:	5	5	5
HDCP:	1	1	3

5

The water tower in the distance is, obviously, what to aim for off the tee. Actually you can aim the second and even the third shot for the tower (that is, if the pin is in the center of the green). The water down the left side really does not come into play until the second shot. The fairway is narrow, so the procedure should be simply to back off and play the shot down the middle. The trees located in the bunkers to the left of the green look pretty, but do not get too close a look! Trees can hinder a backswing, even in a bunker. A large, flat green is very receptive to birdy attempts.

— 23
| 23

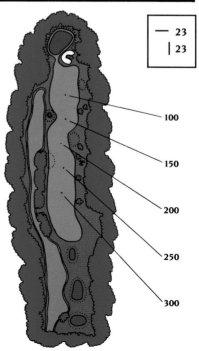

100

150

200

250

300

SEA PINES COUNTRY CLUB

6

	BLUE	WHITE	RED
YDS:	336	328	280
PAR:	4	4	4
HDCP:	11	11	13

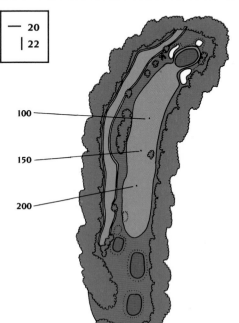

— 20

| 22

100

150

200

A short hole, but challenging nonetheless. First thought is to play the shortest distance, down the right side. However, if you have not learned by now, the trees along the fairways can be very unpleasant. Stay away from trouble and play down the left. A long tee-shot is not required to get into prime location for the approach. Similar to the fourth, this green slopes toward the fairway and can give the illusion of being farther than it actually is. Traps left and right demand an accurate second shot to the putting surface.

A wide fairway is welcome. Left center is still the favored side of the fairway. Longer hitters are advised to back off the long drive because of the water stretching across the fairway up near the green. Trees on the right edge of the fairway can stymie the approach from the right. A large green will give up more two-putts than single putts.

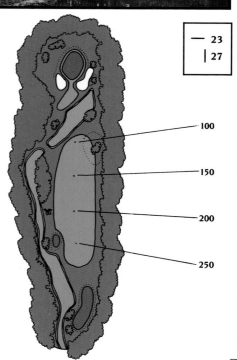

— 23
| 27

100

150

200

250

SEA PINES COUNTRY CLUB

		BLUE	WHITE	RED
8	YDS:	190	176	132
	PAR:	3	3	3
	HDCP:	13	13	15

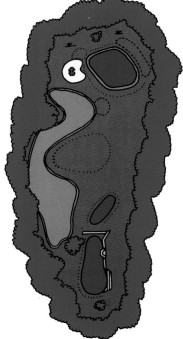

— 23

| 26

Into the wind, this hole can require up to two more clubs than normally used. Play it safe and use the extra length. Water and bunkers short and left will make the 3 that much more difficult to attain. Once on the green, hopefully close to the pin, you will notice the severe slope the putting surface has toward the water. Yikes!!

Wow! This one can look like
a . . .a really difficult hole.
Definitely, it's risky to cut
the corner on this hole. Play
the drive down the left center
of the fairway and expect a
long approach shot. A par 4
on this hole is something
to be proud of.

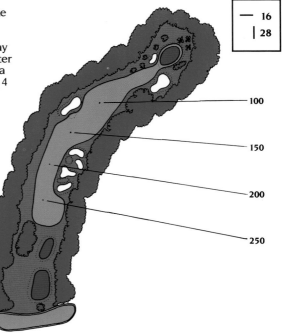

— 16
| 28

100

150

200

250

10		BLUE	WHITE	RED
	YDS:	346	333	283
	PAR:	4	4	4
	HDCP:	14	14	14

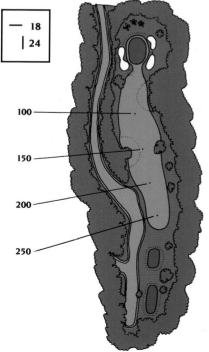

Straightaway, the tenth hole is the perfect hole to start out the back nine. Gentle sloping along the left side will help guide the drives toward the center of the fairway. The approach requires a bit of accuracy to keep clear of the three bunkers surrounding the green. A level putting surface is ideal for the birdie try.

Very short, but again, a test of skill. Trees to left and right guard the green well. A high, lofted shot can be used to find the pin tucked in behind the trees. However, be careful of the wind. Green is longer than it looks. Shots that seem to be accurate are often found quite a distance from the hole.

— 22
| 27

	BLUE	WHITE	RED
YDS:	531	494	409
PAR:	5	5	5
HDCP:	6	6	6

— 24
| 36

100

150

200

250

300

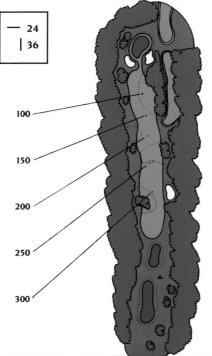

Spanish moss is omnipresent on the twelfth. Aim the drive toward the bunker on the right. Nearly impossible to reach in two, this par 5 should be played in regulation. Play the second shot back toward the left side of the fairway. Notice how the fairway seems to be tightening up. The green is well-protected by a large oak just short and right. An approach to the left center of the green will keep clear of the oak and get the ball to where it needs to be — on the green.

Play the drive down the right center of the fairway. Note that a long drive is not required on this hole. The second shot will be to a green that is elevated and bordered by water to the left and beyond. The putting surface slopes left toward the water but is at a favorable angle for the approach. The sub-par score can be had on this hole.

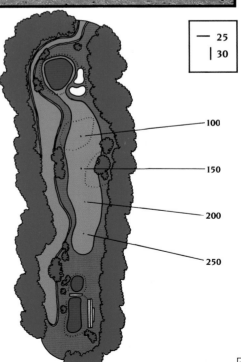

— 25
| 30

100

150

200

250

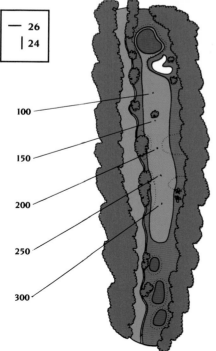

— 26
| 24

100
150
200
250
300

The tree may have been left there as a marker for the center of the fairway, or just an obstacle. Whatever the case, aim for it! There is a choice for the second shot, right or left (or maybe even over!), although the shot is best played to the right. The creek on the left looms into a more formidable adversary closer to the hole.

The large bunker in front of the green is actually about ten yards short of the the putting surface. Be sure to get the ball all the way to the hole on the approach shot.

The fifteenth green is hidden deep within the pines. Bunkers left and right protect the front, and a steep slope beyond discourages the long shot. The center of the green is the only refuge where no trouble is to be found. As always, be careful of the wind above the treeline.

— 26
| 29

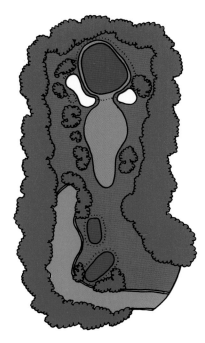

SEA PINES COUNTRY CLUB

16

	BLUE	WHITE	RED
YDS:	373	369	341
PAR:	4	4	4
HDCP:	4	4	4

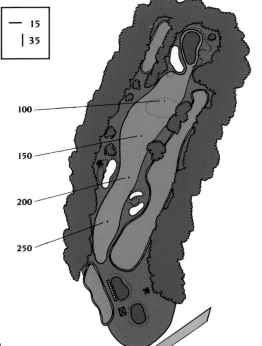

— 15
| 35

100

150

200

250

Do not let the openness of the view from the tee fool you. A lengthy drive down the left side may bound through the fairway into the trees. Bring it back a bit and play just right of the bunker on the left. A two-tiered green is protected by trees and bunker to the left. Obviously, you should play for the right side.

A drive down the right center is advisable to keep well clear of the trees to the left. The green slopes rapidly to the right. Play the approach left of the pin to keep the ball close to the hole, or possibly just below, for an uphill putt.

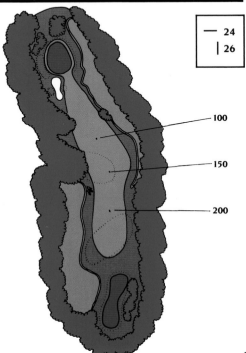

— 24
| 26

100

150

200

SEA PINES COUNTRY CLUB

18

	BLUE	WHITE	RED
YDS:	383	341	297
PAR:	4	4	4
HDCP:	8	8	12

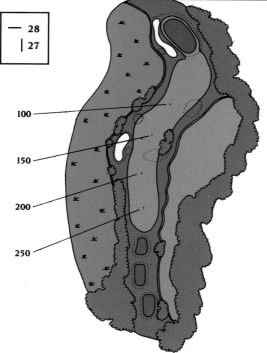

— 28
| 27

100
150
200
250

The ocean has come into view. Marshland to the left of the fairway will indiscriminately add strokes to the score. Play the drive down the left center of the fairway, aiming just right of the bunker to the left. An approach over the marsh is the punishment for a drive too far to the left. The elevated green has bunkers front left and beyond. Upon sinking the final putt, you can recall on this truly difficult golf course that Arnold Palmer has designed.

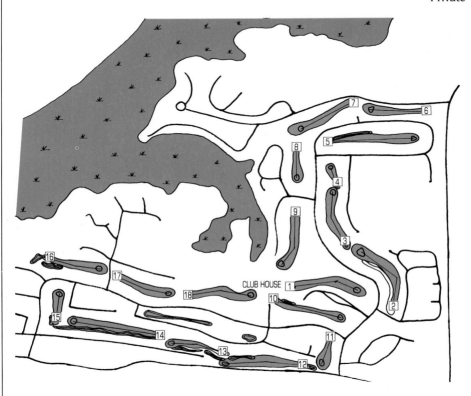

SEA PINES COUNTRY CLUB

Sea Pines Plantation
30 Governors Country Club Drive
Hilton Head Island, SC 29928
803-671-4417
Private

Head Professional: Mike Robinson
Superintendent: Eddie Hipp
Designer: Arnold Palmer

Course	Rating	Slope
Blue	70.7	124
White	69.0	122
Red	70.6	122

HOLE	1	2	3	4	5	6	7	8	9	OUT	10	11	12	13	14	15	16	17	18	IN	TOTAL
BLUE	395	495	345	145	532	336	370	190	370	3178	346	142	531	337	547	160	373	349	383	3168	6346
WHITE	366	483	334	135	490	328	357	176	361	3030	333	134	494	328	515	151	369	342	341	3007	6037
HDCP	3	5	15	17	1	11	7	13	9		14	18	6	12	2	16	4	10	8		
PAR	4	5	4	3	5	4	4	3	4	36	4	3	5	4	5	3	4	4	4	36	72
RED	341	437	318	115	421	280	262	132	315	2621	283	117	409	306	457	125	341	311	297	2646	5267
HDCP	5	1	9	17	3	13	7	15	11		14	18	6	8	2	16	4	10	12		

SHIPYARD PLANTATION

The Plantation

Within the gates of the seemingly tranquil plantation lie 27 holes of championship golf. The 803 acres provides ample space for the golf courses as well as a racquet club featuring 24 tennis courts and a stretch of warm sandy beaches.

The Courses

The Brigantine is the shortest of the three courses in Shipyard. Willard Byrd designed the layout with an over zealous use of water. The first hole utilizes bunkers to create an elusive hole. The following eight not only include fairway bunkers, but also add a bit of water to create a true test of ball control. A good supply of golf balls may be a good idea . . .

The Clipper was designed by George Cobb and is the longest of the three nine-hole courses. At more than 3400 yards, Clipper also has the unique distinction of having one hole without a water hazard, the sixth. The first hole squares off quickly — length coupled with fairway bunkers and a bit of water. Maybe the toughest of the three.

Short, wide fairways greet the golfer on the Galleon. Although water is present on every hole, it should not come into play — unless some wild shots are executed. The layout is short and interesting. Playing the Galleon is both fun and rewarding.

The Shipyard courses are unique in that one can play any two courses in whatever order he or she chooses. The combinations are up to you!

Designer Willard Byrd, produced this beautiful golf course. Aptly named the Brigantine, the course is to other courses as the brigantine vessel is to other sailing ships. A bit out of the ordinary, these nine holes will surely test the skill of all golfers. This first hole starts off with a slight bend to the right. Play the drive just right of the fairway trap; keeping right will allow for a clear shot of the green for the second shot. The approach is made to a flat elevated green guarded by three traps.

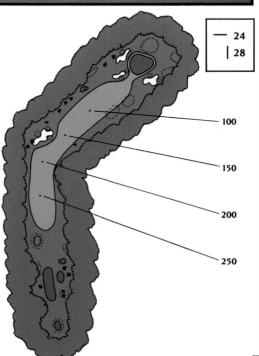

― 24
| 28

100

150

200

250

BRIGANTINE GOLF COURSE

2

	BLUE	WHITE	RED
YDS:	396	359	286
PAR:	4	4	4
HDCP:	3	3	3

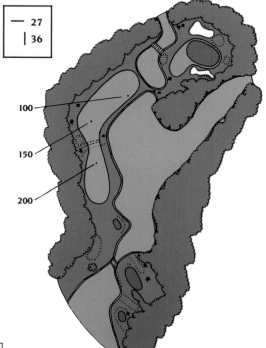

— 27
| 36

100

150

200

This is where you'll be able to see the creativity of the designer. By tucking the tees up in among the trees, the architect has drawn our attention toward the vast stretch of fairway that happens to be bordered by water. As if that were not enough, we have a little dogleg to negotiate! Obviously, the best drive is down the center with a slight fade. Bouncing around the corner, the ball should come to rest just under 140 yards from the flag. Water sneaks in close, and there are trees and traps around the green. So go for the center of the green! Tap in the putt, and on to the next hole!

Hopefully the wind is will not be in your face on this hole. Downwind, it's possible to reach this par 5 in two! Conservatively (but still birdie possbility!), a drive down left center is ideal. Second shot should also be down the left side. Water is still right, so why tempt it? A fairly large green is receptive to all worthy attempts. The green is flat, and a birdie is not out of the question.

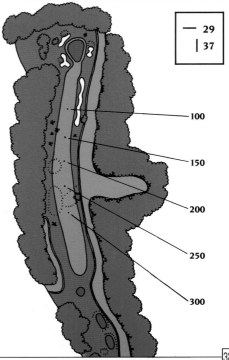

— 29
| 37

100

150

200

250

300

BRIGANTINE GOLF COURSE

4

	BLUE	WHITE	RED
YDS:	347	318	246
PAR:	4	4	4
HDCP:	7	7	6

— 25
| 35

100

150

200

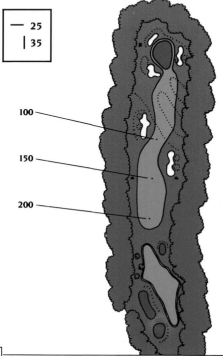

Relatively short, this par 4 is straight away. The fairway bunker on the right is within driving distance. Avoid it by keeping the ball left. Rolling fairway adds a bit of difficulty to this hole. The approach is made to an elevated green surrounded by three bunkers. A crisp shot to the hole may yield a birdie!

BRIGANTINE GOLF COURSE

	BLUE	WHITE	RED
YDS:	173	143	117
PAR:	3	3	3
HDCP:	8	8	8

5

Concentrate on the big green in the foreground. Ignore the water and bunker to the left and keep your attention on the job at hand. A buried elephant (figuratively!) leaves a large mound on most of the green. Sinking the ball in one putt is an accomplishment!

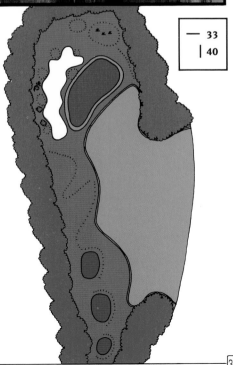

— 33
| 40

BRIGANTINE GOLF COURSE

6

	BLUE	WHITE	RED
YDS:	404	344	266
PAR:	4	4	4
HDCP:	1	1	5

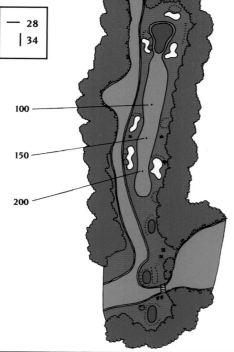

— 28
| 34

100

150

200

Although these types boats are relatively stable, this particular brigantine is keeling on this hole! From all the way back, the hole looks a bit difficult. The tee shot must be directed down the middle of the fairway to avoid possible trouble with water left and trees right. Once negotiated between the fairway bunkers, the second shot will most likely be a long one into the green. Three more bunkers surround the putting surface. Put a good move on the trusty old niblick to get the ball up to the pin.

The fade is favored on this hole. A drive down the fairway should be long enough to get past the big pine on the right. A rolling fairway lies between the drive and the elevated green. A solid approach shot to the center of the green is needed a the chance to make sub-par score on this hole.

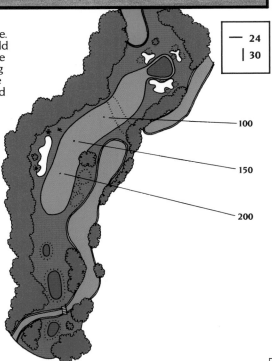

— 24
| 30

100

150

200

BRIGANTINE GOLF COURSE

8

	BLUE	WHITE	RED
YDS:	192	153	127
PAR:	3	3	3
HDCP:	9	9	9

— 20
| 37

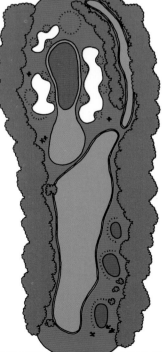

A long, narrow green is the target. Pay special attention to the location of the flagstick. Using the right club for the distance is crucial. Bunkers play havoc around the green; take them in stride. Remember, sand traps are easily exited with a solid stroke through the sand. You, too, can explode the ball onto the green.

Staying down the right side is advised on this hole. Water along the left will gobble up any errant tee shots. The second shot should be played, cautiously, down the left side. It is important to get the ball to the left in order to have a clear approach to the green. One palm tree short right and another inside the curve on the right of the green will rebound seemingly good shots.

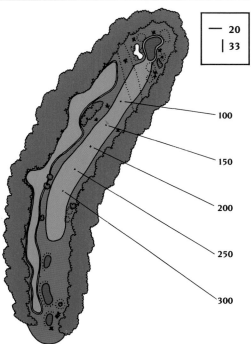

— 20
| 33

100

150

200

250

300

BRIGANTINE/CLIPPER

Shipyard Plantation
P.O. Drawer 7229
Hilton Head Island, SC 29928
803-785-2402
Resort

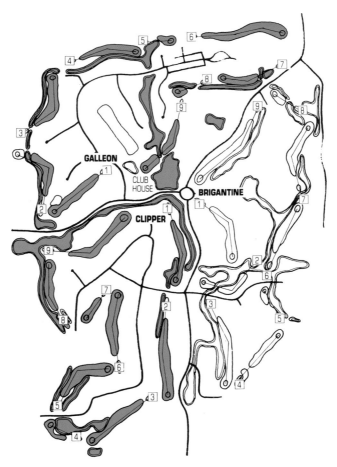

Course	Rating	Slope
Blue	72.9	128
White	68.9	122
Red	70.3	116

Head Professional: Peter J. Rouillard
Superintendent: James M. Norby
Designers: Willard Byrd / George Cobb
Teaching Professional: Ron J. Cerrudo

HOLE	1	2	3	4	5	6	7	8	9	OUT	10	11	12	13	14	15	16	17	18	IN	TOTAL
BLUE	401	396	501	347	173	404	415	192	523	3352	428	567	407	178	380	427	196	366	517	3466	6818
WHITE	347	359	464	318	143	344	349	153	482	2959	370	526	378	147	352	400	144	326	489	3132	6091
HDCP	5	3	6	7	8	1	2	9	4		3	2	4	8	6	1	9	7	5		
PAR	4	4	5	4	3	4	4	3	5	36	4	5	4	3	4	4	3	4	5	36	72
RED	290	286	401	246	117	266	303	127	421	2457	307	466	335	134	300	348	114	307	422	2733	5190
HDCP	7	3	4	6	8	5	2	9	1		5	2	3	8	6	1	9	7	4		

	BLUE	WHITE	RED
YDS:	428	370	307
PAR:	4	4	4
HDCP:	3	3	5

Although the clipper vessel is known for its great speed, it is advised that this course should not be rushed through. The first hole will reveal the character of the holes to come. The target area off the tee should be just right of the fairway bunker on the left. Water right and left may surprise the few who try bending their drives around the dogleg. Hit the approach a bit longer than needed; the trouble lies in front of the putting surface. The slow-rolling green is guaranteed to keep one's attention on putting.

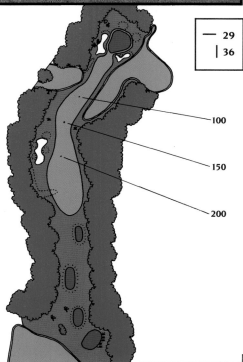

— 29
| 36

100

150

200

CLIPPER GOLF COURSE

2

	BLUE	WHITE	RED
YDS:	567	526	466
PAR:	5	5	5
HDCP:	2	2	2

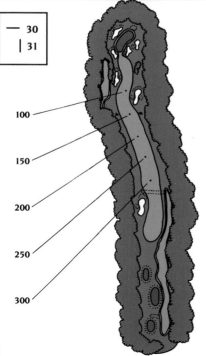

— 30
| 31

100

150

200

250

300

Water along the right side should be of no concern off the tee. A drive down the right center of the fairway will yield good position for the second shot. A second fairway bunker hints that the second shot should be played down the left side. Be careful of the lagoon that sneaks out of the trees. The approach is to a narrow, flat green. Bunkers all around will grab any stray shots. On in three, two putts, and on to the next hole!

A large lagoon creeps in from the right. A long drive is not advised. Bring it down a notch and play a long iron or fairway wood off the tee. Position is the objective. Straight down the middle is about right. The approach is to another elevated green. Bunkers in triangular outline are overshadowed by the large putting surface. If not in on one, be sure to get the first putt close for easy tap-in.

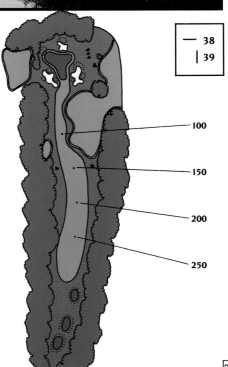

— 38
| 39

100

150

200

250

CLIPPER GOLF COURSE

4

	BLUE	WHITE	RED
YDS:	178	147	134
PAR:	3	3	3
HDCP:	8	8	8

— 34
| 31

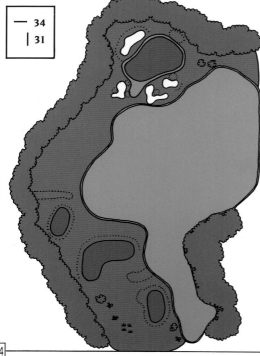

As if just getting the ball over the water were not difficult enough! Club selection is of vital importance. Once clearing the lagoon, the ball must be directed over bunkers to an elevated green. A strong wind could influence club choice by at least three clubs! Short is definitely trouble, and long is out of bounds, so simply hit the ball onto the green!

If the fourth did not go as planned, the fifth is where lost ground can be made up. A long iron or fairway wood is the club to use off the tee. Play the ball down the middle, better to the left than right if it must stray. The longer hitter may want to cut the corner to set up for a short chip to the green. Hit the second shot solidly to get up close to the pin for the tap-in birdie! Remember, this Clipper can move quickly — so be sure to stay with the game.

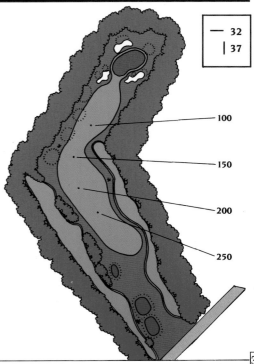

— 32
| 37

100

150

200

250

CLIPPER GOLF COURSE

6

	BLUE	WHITE	RED
YDS:	427	400	348
PAR:	4	4	4
HDCP:	1	1	1

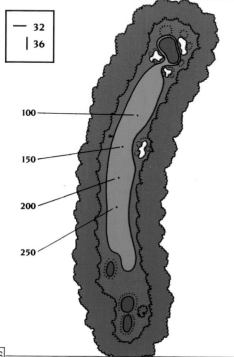

— 32
| 36

100
150
200
250

No more fun. This sixth hole is a demanding par 4. A well-hit drive up the right center is required to establish a good chance at getting to the green on the second shot. Bunker short right is misleading; do not veer left. Keep the approach a bit down the right side, as the large trap to the left is a greedy monster. The large putting surface will add to the challenge of getting the ball down in two.

	BLUE	WHITE	RED
YDS:	196	144	114
PAR:	3	3	3
HDCP:	9	9	9

7

Fairly long from all the way back, this par three is not deceiving. It is as difficult as it looks. Four bunkers surround the putting surface. Observation of the pin location is important when choosing the correct club. A 3 here is admirable!

— 23
| 42

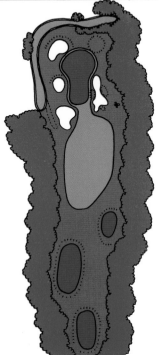

CLIPPER GOLF COURSE

8

	BLUE	WHITE	RED
YDS:	366	326	307
PAR:	4	4	4
HDCP:	7	7	7

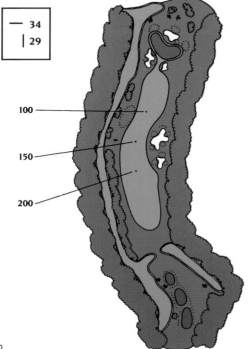

— 34
| 29

100

150

200

A slight dogleg to the right, this eighth hole can be used to get back into the game. A drive down the left center will set up a good second shot. The approach is to an elevated green. Slight rolling on the putting surface will test the accuracy of the putter. The objective is to get some shots back, so drain the putt!

CLIPPER GOLF COURSE

	BLUE	WHITE	RED
YDS:	517	489	422
PAR:	5	5	5
HDCP:	5	5	4

9

Homestretch! A well-hit drive down the middle is always a happy event. Fairway bunkers — one left and two right — are within driving range. A peek around the corner will reveal a landscape filled with bunkers! Play the second shot down the left side. The third shot should be hit with the intention of holing the ball! The wide green is lost in the crowd of bunkers. If the putter is still hot, go ahead and make the putt. A pat on the back is in order; this is a tough course!

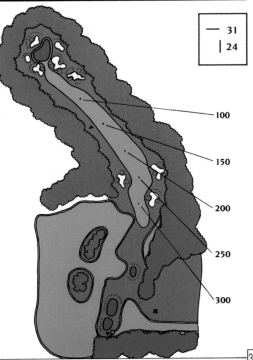

— 31
| 24

100
150
200
250
300

CLIPPER / GALLEON

Shipyard Plantation
P.O. Drawer 7229
Hilton Head Island, SC 29928
803-785-2402
Resort

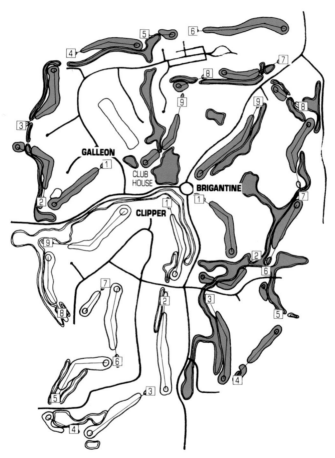

Course	Rating	Slope
Blue	73.3	129
White	69.9	123
Red	71.6	119

Head Professional: Peter J. Rouillard
Superintendent: James M. Norby
Designer: George Cobb
Teaching Professional: Ron J. Cerrudo

HOLE	1	2	3	4	5	6	7	8	9	OUT	10	11	12	13	14	15	16	17	18	IN	TOTAL
BLUE	428	567	407	178	380	427	196	366	517	3466	393	477	418	407	179	517	384	179	410	3364	6830
WHITE	370	526	378	147	352	400	144	326	489	3132	359	445	381	373	144	480	336	146	371	3035	6167
HDCP	3	2	4	8	6	1	9	7	5		7	6	1	4	8	2	5	9	3		
PAR	4	5	4	3	4	4	3	4	5	36	4	5	4	4	3	5	4	3	4	36	72
RED	307	466	335	134	300	348	114	307	422	2733	315	408	335	343	113	409	313	121	301	2658	5391
HDCP	5	2	3	8	6	1	9	7	4		6	3	2	4	9	1	5	8	7		

This first hole of the Galleon course starts the nine with authority. It quickly becomes apparent that this is serious golf. Three bunkers loom just off the tee, awaiting the errant tee shot. Water sneaks in from the right side, while two more deep bunkers lie ominously in front of the green.

Play the drive down the left middle of the fairway. The approach must be strong and long enough. The two front bunkers can put a damper on the easy par. Start the day off smartly, and play the approach to the heart of the green.

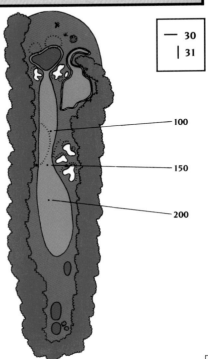

— 30
| 31

100

150

200

GALLEON GOLF COURSE

2

	BLUE	WHITE	RED
YDS:	477	445	408
PAR:	5	5	5
HDCP:	6	6	3

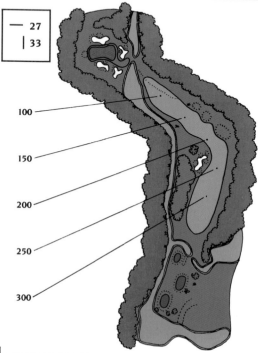

— 27
| 33

100
150
200
250
300

This second hole is not very long and would be fairly easy to target in two if the fairway were straight. Unfortunately, the hole takes a severe turn to the left. Water is all around. The water bleeds in from the right side and continues up the left side for another crossing of the fairway. Keeping the ball dry is imperative for the par.

Play the drive down the right center of the fairway, setting up for the second to lay up just short of the water. The third shot should follow up to the center of the green. Planning on two putts will guarantee the par on this front sloping-green.

This third hole demands both accuracy and length. A mighty drive down the right center of the fairway is a must for the approach. Three bunkers, to the right, increases the difficulty of the second shot and, possibly, the par.

The approach is to a slightly elevated green. Two bunkers, left and right, will happily grab any shots that stray off line. The putting surface is somewhat flat and level, allowing for most putts to be made on the first attempt.

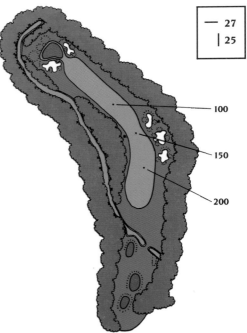

— 27
| 25

100

150

200

343

	BLUE	WHITE	RED
YDS:	407	373	343
PAR:	4	4	4
HDCP:	4	4	4

— 24
| 32

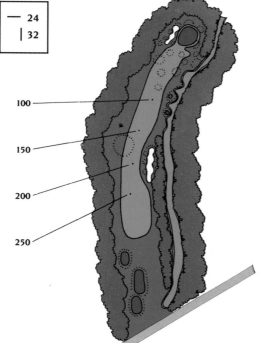

100

150

200

250

Shorter than the third, but just as tough. Water curves all the way up the right side, but only causes problems for shots that are sent far to the right. Only one fairway bunker and one greenside bunker are situated on this hole, but their presence is to more for the sake of guidance than hindrance.

The drive should be played down the left side of the fairway. This will open up the green for the approach. A medium-length second shot should be aimed toward the right side of the green. Par will keep pace with the competition.

	BLUE	WHITE	RED
YDS:	179	144	113
PAR:	3	3	3
HDCP:	8	8	9

5

The first par 3 is introduced with no subtlety whatsoever. The teeing area is tucked in amongst the trees, while the green is encircled by pines and bunkers. A solid tee shot is necessary to keep the ball dry and on course.

The putting surface is fairly flat, allowing for easy putting.

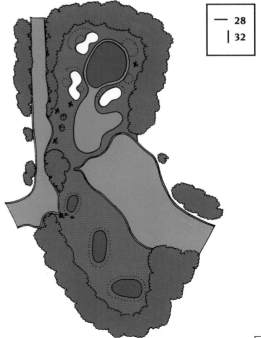

— 28
| 32

GALLEON GOLF COURSE

6	BLUE	WHITE	RED
YDS:	517	480	409
PAR:	5	5	5
HDCP:	2	2	1

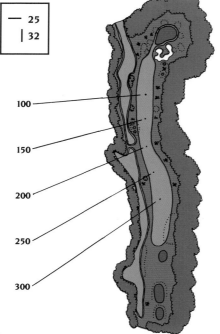

— 25

| 32

100
150
200
250
300

Those who hit the ball left will not enjoy this hole; water parallels the entire length of the fairway. A drive down the right side is desirable. The second shot should be played down the middle to the left side.

The approach must carry the large bunker which stands guard over the green. The large putting surface slopes down from the back, giving the illusion of being smaller and further than it actually is.

GALLEON GOLF COURSE

	BLUE	WHITE	RED
YDS:	384	336	313
PAR:	4	4	4
HDCP:	5	5	5

7

The tees are slightly elevated and look outward to a fairway that slopes away toward the green. A drive that sails down the left center of the fairway, coming to rest 150 yards from the green, will be in perfect position for the approach.

The green is long and narrow, proving to be a difficult target for the second shot. Two bunkers sweep in from the right, while one lone bunker backs up the left side. Accuracy is needed to get the ball safely onto the putting surface.

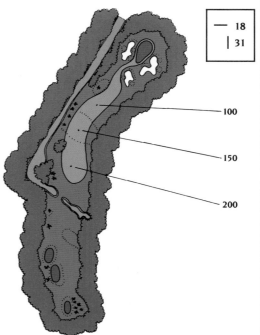

— 18
| 31

100

150

200

GALLEON GOLF COURSE

8

	BLUE	WHITE	RED
YDS:	179	146	121
PAR:	3	3	3
HDCP:	9	9	8

```
— 33
| 35
```

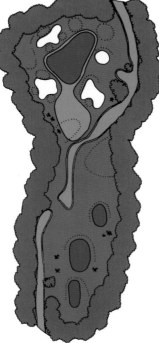

The ground slopes away from the tees to a lagoon which swells from the left to flow around the green. Bunkers are situated on the all four corners of the green. A tee shot must be played to the center of the green for any hope of birdie.

GALLEON GOLF COURSE

	BLUE	WHITE	RED
YDS:	410	371	301
PAR:	4	4	4
HDCP:	3	3	7

9

The clubhouse is in view, but the round is far from finished. This ninth hole demands the undivided attention of the golfer. Water comes in from the right and meanders across the fairway to the left. A smashing drive along the left side of the fairway is a necessity.

The approach shot must avoid the bunkers and fall close to the cup. The crowd up on the deck of the clubhouse will wonder who that great golfer is when they see you place the second shot delicately onto the putting surface. Tap the ball in and pencil in the birdie on the scorecard. The Galleon has been successfully completed!

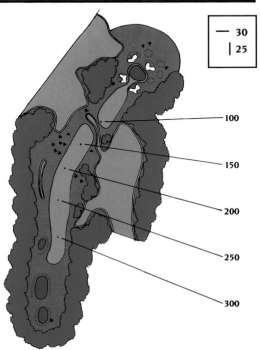

BRIGANTINE/GALLEON

Shipyard Plantation
P.O. Drawer 7229
Hilton Head Island, SC 29928
803-785-2402
Resort

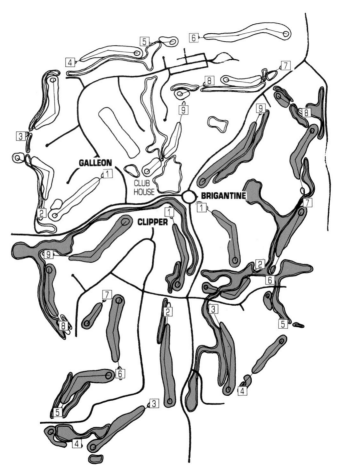

Course	Rating	Slope
Blue	72.6	128
White	69.3	120
Red	69.9	114

Head Professional: Peter J. Rouillard
Superintendent: James M. Norby
Designers: Willard Byrd / George Cobb
Teaching Professional: Ron J. Cerrudo

HOLE	1	2	3	4	5	6	7	8	9	OUT	10	11	12	13	14	15	16	17	18	IN	TOTAL
BLUE	401	396	501	347	173	404	415	192	523	3352	393	477	418	407	179	517	384	179	410	3364	6716
WHITE	347	359	464	318	143	344	349	153	482	2959	359	445	381	373	144	480	336	146	371	3035	5994
HDCP	5	3	6	7	8	1	2	9	4		7	6	1	4	8	2	5	9	3		
PAR	4	4	5	4	3	4	4	3	5	36	4	5	4	4	3	5	4	3	4	36	72
RED	290	286	401	246	117	266	303	127	421	2457	315	408	335	343	113	409	313	121	301	2658	5115
HDCP	7	3	4	6	8	5	2	9	1		6	3	2	4	9	1	5	8	7		

SPANISH WELLS GOLF CLUB

The Course

Located in a remote spot on Hilton Head Island, the Spanish Wells Golf Club is hidden from the more populated areas. Since it was built in 1969, it's surprising that few are even aware of the existence of one of the more enjoyable courses on the island. The George Cobb-designed layout features wide fairways which run smooth and gentle up to the elevated, undulating greens. Tee shots are forgiven, but the putting surfaces will be a good match for the putter. Although length is not the main concern, an emphasis on ball control and accuracy is important in order to reach the greens safely.

The front nine actually doubles for the back nine in this nine-hole design. Different tee markers are used to distinguish the front nine from the back nine. The front nine begins with a short par 4, possibly yielding an early birdie. The second brings things back to reality, a par 4 at 403 yards for the men. The first nine holes can prove to be rewarding, boosting hopes for the back nine.

The turn to the back side is not simply a replay of the front. The men will now play the Blue tees instead of the Whites, and the women will play the Gold instead of the Red. Different angles, and slightly different yardages, allow for variation in the layout. The eleventh hole becomes a par 5 at 502 yards. (Birdie probabilities are high.) As the front nine turned in at par 36, so does the back, giving a total par of 72 on this unique nine-hole layout.

SPANISH WELLS GOLF CLUB

	WHITE	RED	BLUE	GOLD
YDS:	331	269	344	283
PAR:	4	4	4	4
HDCP:	13	13	14	14

1

The course starts off with a fairly easy par 4. Peeking through the pines, you'll be able to see the green. Dogleg right and fairly short, this hole can inspire optimism. Simply play the drive down the middle of the fairway. The approach is made by going right for the pin; (Might as well start off strong!) The long green gives the illusion that the flag is closer than it actually is. Traps left and right stand guard, but the hole is easily accessible.

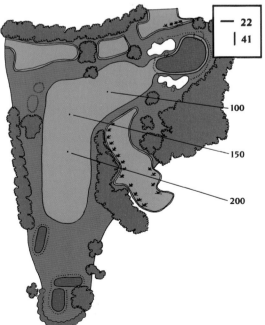

SPANISH WELLS GOLF CLUB

2

	WHITE	RED	BLUE	GOLD
YDS:	403	336	502	377
PAR:	4	4	5	5
HDCP:	1	1	8	8

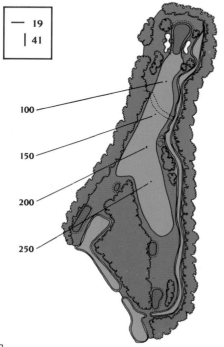

```
— 19
| 41
```

100

150

200

250

A long par 4 for the second, but a short par 5 for the eleventh. This hole is a good solid challenge from either tee. The second plays a slight dogleg left. Coming out of the chute, which is created by trees left and right, take care to get the drive out into play. The approach shot may be long to an open green that is relatively flat. A 4 on this hole is admirable. The par 5 eleventh hole is a good birdie hole. A slight dogleg right, this hole can be reached in two. Eagles are possible. However, a par is acceptable.

SPANISH WELLS GOLF CLUB

	WHITE	RED	BLUE	GOLD
YDS:	442	335	355	300
PAR:	5	5	4	4
HDCP:	7	7	6	10

3

The third is a very short par five that must be completed in par or less. Dogleg right and large open fairway will create the urge to hit the drive big and down the right side. Although a par 5, it is not neccessary to cut the corner on this hole. Play the drive down the middle to be in good position for the second shot and well clear of trees along the right. The approaches for both the twelfth and the third are made to an elevated green. Bunkers in front look frightfully large. Keeping clear will help to avoid any unwanted strokes.

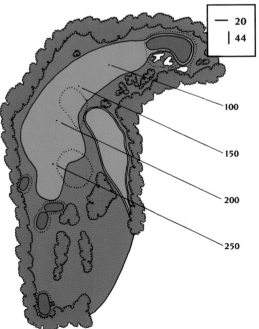

20

44

100

150

200

250

	WHITE	RED	BLUE	GOLD
YDS:	184	118	168	152
PAR:	3	3	3	3
HDCP:	15	17	18	16

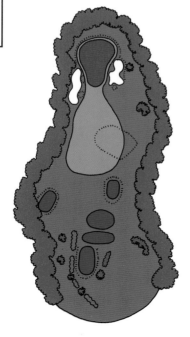

— 19
| 35

The fourth hole white tees are longer than the thirteenth blue tees, but the fourth red are shorter than the thirteenth gold. Solid par 3 from any tee, this hole is well-protected around the green. Be careful of the wind above the treeline. As with all par threes, a par is definitely a good score.

SPANISH WELLS GOLF CLUB

	WHITE	RED	BLUE	GOLD
YDS:	378	323	365	316
PAR:	4	4	4	4
HDCP:	5	5	4	6

5

The fifth is just a slight dogleg to the left. The rolling fairway slopes to the right. A wide-open fairway begs for the big drive. Usually into the wind, this par four can be surprising. Play smart and keep the ball down the center. An approach is made to a large green which also slopes to the right. Bunkers short left and back right will attract any stray shots.

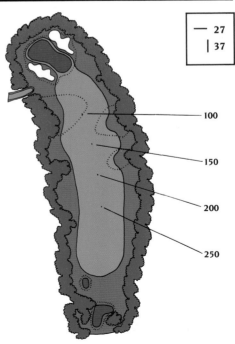

— 27

| 37

100

150

200

250

SPANISH WELLS GOLF CLUB

6

	WHITE	RED	BLUE	GOLD
YDS:	346	300	362	307
PAR:	4	4	4	4
HDCP:	3	3	2	2

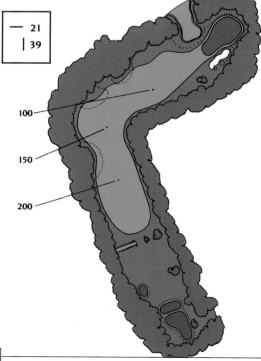

— 21
| 39

100

150

200

From the tee, the green is not visible. The hole cuts sharply to the right. Although it is ideal to play for the far side of the fairway, it is not necessary to hit the ball far. Play a long iron or fairway wood off the tee. The approach to the green is made from the corner of the dogleg. The trees crowd into view. Accuracy is a must. A deep pond sits just short and left of the green. Any balls rolling near it will be pulled into the drink. The putting surface is two-tiered, sloping from back to front. Keep the ball below the hole for the uphill putt.

SPANISH WELLS GOLF CLUB

	WHITE	RED	BLUE	GOLD
YDS:	425	379	448	372
PAR:	5	5	5	5
HDCP:	9	9	10	12

7

Big hitters will enjoy this hole. Cutting the corner is very possible, believe it or not! With the wind blowing left to right, a well-hit shot just over the corner will find its way well down the fairway. A safe and conservative route will be straight down the middle. Be careful, though. The fairway turns right about 210 yards out. The long narrow green slopes forward, dropping down three levels. Note the position of the flag for the correct club selection. Birdies are in the air!

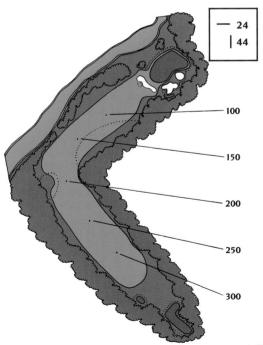

— 24
| 44

100

150

200

250

300

SPANISH WELLS GOLF CLUB

8

	WHITE	RED	BLUE	GOLD
YDS:	152	134	171	118
PAR:	3	3	3	3
HDCP:	17	15	16	18

— 20
| 38

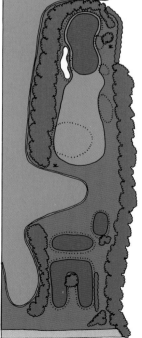

The eighth hole plays a bit shorter than the seventeenth. A small pond in front of the tee must be transited to get to the green, which is long and narrow. Careful club selection is important.

SPANISH WELLS GOLF CLUB

	WHITE	RED	BLUE	GOLD
YDS:	345	277	364	345
PAR:	4	4	4	4
HDCP:	11	11	12	4

9

From the back tees the vista is intimidating. The drive must be played out of a chute to a seemingly tight fairway. Fairway bunkers to the right are targets you don't want to hit, so play the drive just left of them. A stray shot 'way to the right may find the water, but the water should not be part of the activity if the hole is played correctly. The flat, level green is receptive to accurate second shots. Roll the putt in on the first try, and finish the day with a birdie!

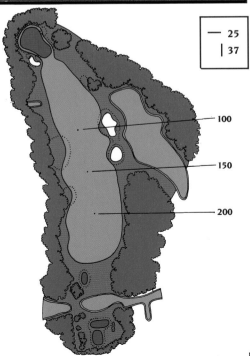

— 25
| 37

100

150

200

SPANISH WELLS GOLF CLUB

Spanish Wells
One Brams Point Road
Hilton Head Island, S.C. 29926
803-681-2819
Private

CLUB HOUSE

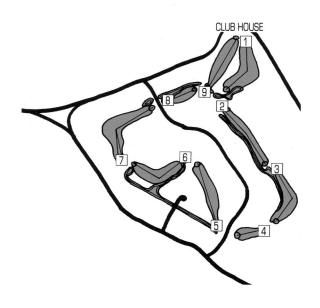

Head Professional: Ted Wells
Superintendent: Ted Wells
Designer: George Cobb

Course	Rating	Slope
White	69.2	119
Red	69.0	111

HOLE	1	2	3	4	5	6	7	8	9	OUT	10	11	12	13	14	15	16	17	18	IN	TOTAL
WHITE	331	403	442	184	378	346	425	152	345	3006	344	502	355	168	365	362	448	171	364	3079	6085
HDCP	13	1	7	15	5	3	9	17	11		14	8	6	18	4	2	10	16	12		
PAR	4	4	5	3	4	4	5	3	4	36	4	5	4	3	4	4	5	3	4	36	72
RED	269	336	335	118	323	300	379	134	277	2471	283	377	300	152	316	307	372	118	345	2570	5041
HDCP	13	1	7	17	5	3	9	15	11		14	8	10	16	6	2	12	18	4		

WEXFORD PLANTATION

The Plantation

At 500 acres, Wexford Plantation is the island's smallest plantation. However, size is not everything. Wexford offers a very unique design. One of the more interesting features of the Wexford Plantation are the unique waterways which weave throughout and are controlled by a private lock system. These waterways provide the homeowners the opportunity to park their yachts only footsteps from their backdoors.

The Course

Designed by Willard C. Byrd, the Wexford golf course opened for play in October of 1989. The course quickly became respected among the golfing community as being a very challenging golf and beautiful golf course.

The Wexford golf course can play as long as 6900 yards from the professional tees and a good 5200 yards from the women's tees. The front nine will prove in a hurry that this golf course demands accuracy. The heavily wooded fairways are best played from the center. Any stray from the fairway will find the pines. From that point a simple chipshot back to the fairway is advised; some risky attempts have a habit of causing only more trouble. The ninth hole brings the golfer out from the pines for a harbourside view.

The back nine turns out for a view of Broad Creek. The first few holes are long and tight. The last few holes are not too long, but the marshlands come into play. Spectacular views as well as golf can be found within the Wexford Plantation.

WEXFORD GOLF CLUB

	BLUE	WHITE	GREEN	RED
YDS:	378	359	332	300
PAR:	4	4	4	4
HDCP:	13	13	13	13

1

The first hole starts off straight. Bunkers along the left side of the fairway will encourage drives to the right. Gentle mounding down the right may help to coax errant balls back to the center. The necessity for accuracy is obvious at the approach. The putting surface slopes back to front, creating the possibility of some tricky down-hill putts if the shot to the green is beyond the flag. Keeping the ball short of the hole will insure an uphill putt.

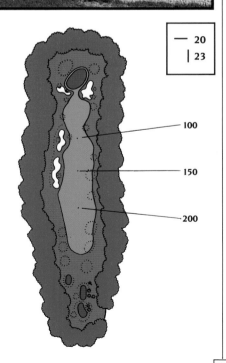

— 20
| 23

100

150

200

WEXFORD GOLF CLUB

2

	BLUE	WHITE	GREEN	RED
YDS:	404	383	355	327
PAR:	4	4	4	4
HDCP:	9	9	9	11

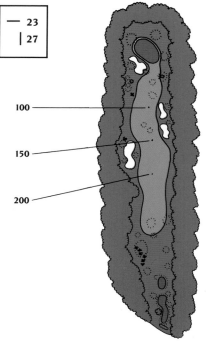

— 23
| 27

100

150

200

On this second hole, Willard Byrd throws new, challenging elements into the game. A long narrow fairway tightens the nerves. The line of trees along the right dictates drives toward the left, but be careful. Fairway bunkers are waiting patiently. A solid drive down the right middle will set up for the approach. A long second shot can be expected.

The undulating fairway leads up to a fairly small green. Cut between mounding left and pines right, the green is fronted by a large bunker. Once on the putting surface, putts should drop on the first attempt.

WEXFORD GOLF CLUB

	BLUE	WHITE	GREEN	RED
YDS:	177	158	140	120
PAR:	3	3	3	3
HDCP:	17	17	17	15

3

The third is not a long par 3, but it can be tricky. Cut deep within the trees, the hole mandates accuracy off the tee. A pond sneaks in from the left, while pines line the right. Bunkers are front left, and beyond. The putting surface sits in silence, awaiting its visitors. Par 3 is a must — although birdies are not out of the question.

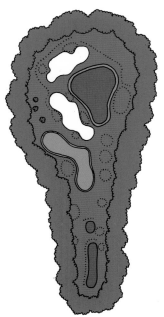

— 23
| 34

WEXFORD GOLF CLUB

4

	BLUE	WHITE	GREEN	RED
YDS:	418	389	353	335
PAR:	4	4	4	4
HDCP:	3	3	3	7

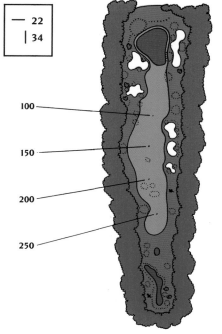

— 22
| 34

100
150
200
250

From the back tees, the view down the fairway is tight. Two good shots are required to get to the green. Fairway bunkers along the right are all too easily. Play the drive down the left middle. A second shot, picked cleanly off the turf, should be aimed for the center of the green. The putting surface slopes slightly to the right. Care should be taken to avoid bunkers on the left.

WEXFORD GOLF CLUB

	BLUE	WHITE	GREEN	RED
YDS:	542	514	487	452
PAR:	5	5	5	5
HDCP:	3	3	3	7

5

On this fifth hole, the fairway opens up for the drive off the tee. For the second shot, however, the fairway funnels down to 15 yards wide. Obviously, the second shot must be played with accuracy.

Finally, the fairway opens back up for the green. Unfortunately, a pond sits between the second shot and the flag. Bunkers help to protect the green. The major concern is to get the ball close to the hole on the approach. Any shots to the left back corner will have a slippery downhill putt to the cup. In contrast, shots to the right front will make for an easier uphill putt.

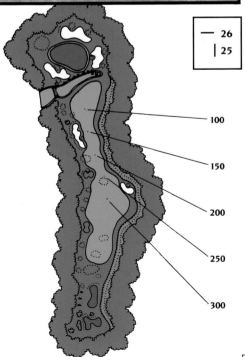

WEXFORD GOLF CLUB

6

	BLUE	WHITE	GREEN	RED
YDS:	170	153	138	121
PAR:	3	3	3	3
HDCP:	15	15	15	17

— 18
| 38

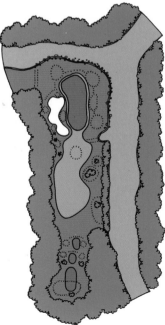

The sixth is a good par 3. The tee is cut back among the pines. This pocket of trees opens up as you get nearer to the green. The putting surface elevates to the back. Long and narrow, the green sets the stage for some long, tricky putts.

A solid shot off the tee should be played carefully. The open green is unprotected from strong winds. Usually right to left, the wind may not be noticed from the tee. Pay attention to the direction in which the flag is blowing, and play accordingly.

WEXFORD GOLF CLUB

	BLUE	WHITE	GREEN	RED
YDS:	378	364	341	296
PAR:	4	4	4	4
HDCP:	11	11	11	9

7

This seventh hole requires a bit of discretion with the tee shot. Much of the fairway is not visible from the tee. The fairway bunkers, however, can be seen to the right. A drive down the left middle will place the ball in an ideal position for the approach.

The serpentine-shaped green can be tough to hit. Keep the ball to the center. Bunkers left and right will add difficulty to a par. Get the first putt close to the hole so that the second will be an easy tap-in.

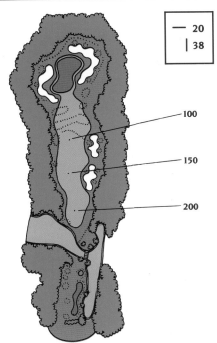

— 20
| 38

100

150

200

WEXFORD GOLF CLUB

8

	BLUE	WHITE	GREEN	RED
YDS:	545	507	480	444
PAR:	5	5	5	5
HDCP:	5	5	5	3

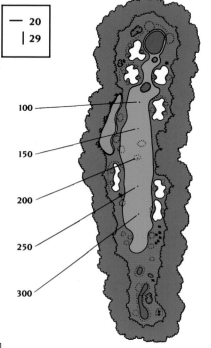

— 20

| 29

100

150

200

250

300

This par 5 is a bit longer than the fifth hole. A good drive down the left center will insure good positioning. Water comes in from the left near the second shot landing area. Keep the ball right, but out of the bunkers!

The approach is to a fairly large green. Mounding in front gives the illusion that the green is closer than it actually is. Be sure to use enough club. Most shots that are not hit long enough do not make it to the hole!

WEXFORD GOLF CLUB

	BLUE	WHITE	GREEN	RED
YDS:	389	366	340	332
PAR:	4	4	4	4
HDCP:	7	7	7	5

9

One of the more treacherous holes on the course. Undoubtedly, going to the right is not a smart option on this hole. Just a little right and the sand is in play. More to the right and you'll need a boat! Play the drive for the bunker located along the left side. A gentle fade would accentuate the shot well.

The approach is to an elevated, two-tiered green with bunkers left and right. The percentages say to play for the center of the putting surface. It is, however, not necessary to use the sand.

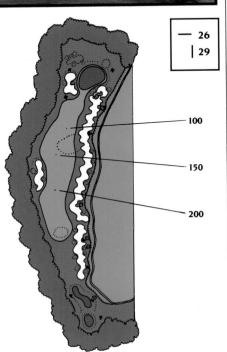

— 26
| 29

100

150

200

WEXFORD GOLF CLUB

10

	BLUE	WHITE	GREEN	RED
YDS:	412	391	336	288
PAR:	4	4	4	4
HDCP:	8	8	8	10

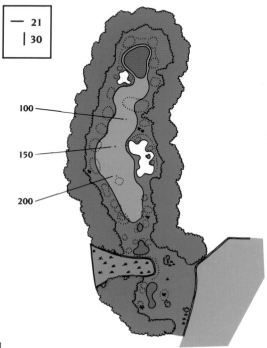

— 21
| 30

100

150

200

The back side starts off with a view of Broad Creek, but the water does not come into play until the seventeenth, and the marsh comes into play only for a brief moment. From the tee, the shot to the fairway seems tight. (Note picture.) The bunker off to the right will discourage any attempts at cutting the dogleg. A mighty drive down the center of the fairway will start the back nine in good stride.

The approach is to a green fronted by a bunker just left. Mounding around the putting surface centers attention on the hole.

WEXFORD GOLF CLUB

	BLUE	WHITE	GREEN	RED
YDS:	558	525	491	445
PAR:	5	5	5	5
HDCP:	6	6	6	4

11

The eleventh is a long par 5. Two large fairway bunkers, left and right, are within driving distance, making a solid drive to the center of the fairway a necessity.

The second shot must be played partially over the water and to the right of the bunker. A third shot of approximately 150 yards should be left to get to the green. One lonely bunker lies short and right of the putting surface. A birdie on this hole should easily beat the competition.

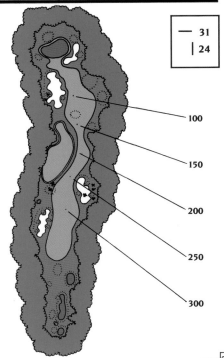

— 31
| 24

100

150

200

250

300

WEXFORD GOLF CLUB

12

	BLUE	WHITE	GREEN	RED
YDS:	442	409	353	287
PAR:	4	4	4	4
HDCP:	4	4	4	12

— 26
| 32

100

150

200

250

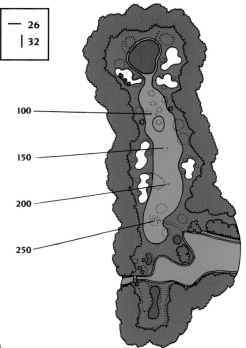

The longest par 4 on the course is also well stocked with bunkers. Three fairway bunkers greet the drive, which must be played carefully off the tee to avoid the water and trees as well. Once in a position to go for the green, the golfer will then notice three more greenside bunkers to contend with. Long, rather than short, is favored here, since the mounding beyond will help stop the ball if it is too long. Any shots left short will most likely find the sand.

WEXFORD GOLF CLUB

	BLUE	WHITE	GREEN	RED
YDS:	162	142	122	94
PAR:	3	3	3	3
HDCP:	18	18	18	18

13

The thirteenth is simple enough. A single pine to the right comes in toward the line of play. Although the hole is not too long, it is important to note the position of the flag. The long narrow green can make the hole play as much as two clubs different. A grass bunker will catch stray shots to the left, while two bunkers sit patiently to the right side. Put the hazards out of mind, and simply hit the ball to the center of the green.

— 17
| 32

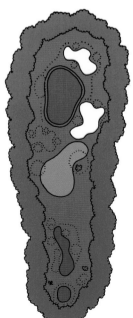

WEXFORD GOLF CLUB

14

	BLUE	WHITE	GREEN	RED
YDS:	381	352	334	294
PAR:	4	4	4	4
HDCP:	16	16	16	14

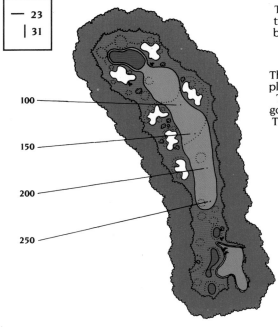

— 23
| 31

100

150

200

250

The fourteenth is similar to the twelfth, only not as long. Three bunkers line the left side of the fairway requiring a straight drive off the tee.

The fairway slopes down off of a plateau from about 90 yards out. This elevated area allows for a good view of the putting surface. The approach shot to the green must avoid the bunkers and fall close to the cup.

WEXFORD GOLF CLUB

	BLUE	WHITE	GREEN	RED
YDS:	554	525	488	444
PAR:	5	5	5	5
HDCP:	2	2	2	2

15

If the driver has been uncontrollable up to this point, it may be well advised to use another club that will keep the ball in the center of the fairway. A bunker just down along the left side is within driving distance.

The second shot should be played down the right side — avoiding the bunker to the right. Be sure to keep to the right because of the water, which comes into play along the left side. A long second shot, although straight down the right middle, may find the rough that has been established by creative grass cutting

The green is cut in among the pines. An accurate shot is a must to get the ball over the water and onto the putting surface. A par 5 will definitely keep the game alive.

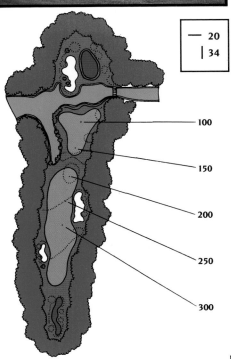

— 20
| 34

100

150

200

250

300

WEXFORD GOLF CLUB

16

	BLUE	WHITE	GREEN	RED
YDS:	410	370	330	308
PAR:	4	4	4	4
HDCP:	10	10	10	8

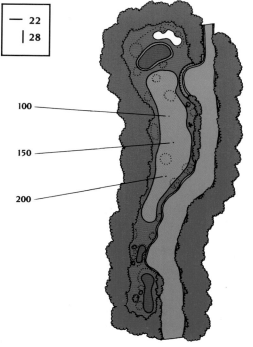

The water from the fifteenth has continued on to the sixteenth. Rolling along the right side, it is apparent that slices will not be tolerated. Keep the drive left and in the fairway.

Only one lone bunker is found beyond the green, but a strong approach will be needed to fight the ever-present headwind. The short, wide putting surface is capable of yielding one-putts.

WEXFORD GOLF CLUB

	BLUE	WHITE	GREEN	RED
YDS:	187	175	141	120
PAR:	3	3	3	3
HDCP:	14	14	14	16

17

The intercoastal is now off to the right, bringing the marshland into play. As if that were not enough, four greenside bunkers sit eagerly awaiting visitors. Careful study of wind and pin placement is of vital importance to get the ball onto the putting surface. A birdie 2 will, without a doubt, win the honors at the next, and final, hole.

— 26
| 29

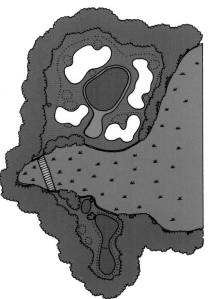

WEXFORD GOLF CLUB

18

	BLUE	WHITE	GREEN	RED
YDS:	380	312	281	225
PAR:	4	4	4	4
HDCP:	12	12	12	6

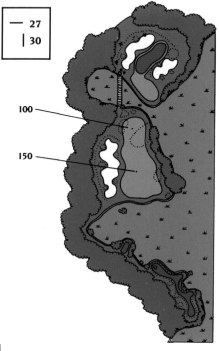

— 27
| 30

100

150

Even the gentlest breeze will cause most golfers to tighten their grip upon address. A good solid drive is required to carry as much as 200 yards of marsh from the back tees. Relax, and swing smoothly — aiming just right of the fairway bunker on the left.

Although the drive has safely found the fairway, the job is not yet completed. The marsh comes back into play for the approach!

The illusive putting surface is elevated and protected by bunkers short right and back left. The surface slopes rapidly from right to left, so slippery sidehill-downhill putts can be expected. Playing smart and conservatively on this last hole is advised if you want to keep the final score to a minimum.

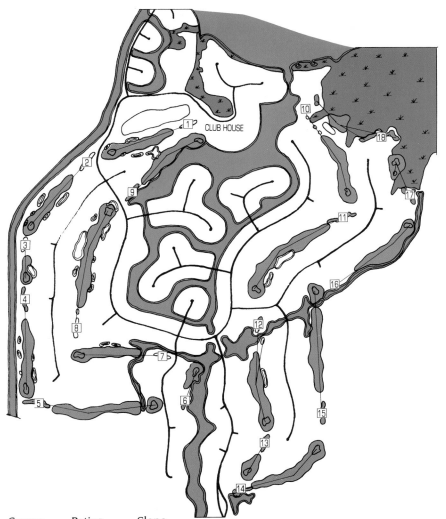

WEXFORD GOLF CLUB

CLUB HOUSE

Course	Rating	Slope
Blue	73.2	125
White	71.1	123
Green	68.4	120
Red	70.0	117

Head Professional: Kieth Goodacher
Superintendent: DeWitt Norby
Designer: Willard Byrd

HOLE	1	2	3	4	5	6	7	8	9	OUT	10	11	12	13	14	15	16	17	18	IN	TOTAL
BLUE	378	404	177	418	542	170	378	545	389	3401	412	558	442	162	381	554	410	187	380	3486	6887
WHITE	359	383	158	389	514	153	364	507	366	3193	391	525	409	142	352	525	370	175	312	3201	6394
GREEN	332	355	140	353	487	138	341	480	340	2966	336	491	353	122	334	488	330	141	281	2876	5842
HDCP	13	9	17	3	1	15	11	5	7		8	6	4	18	16	2	10	14	12		
PAR	4	4	3	4	5	3	4	5	4	36	4	5	4	3	4	5	4	3	4	36	72
RED	300	327	120	335	452	121	296	444	332	2727	288	445	287	94	294	444	308	120	225	2505	5232
HDCP	13	11	15	7	1	17	9	3	5		10	4	12	18	14	2	8	16	6		

The Facts

The aggregation of golf holes on Hilton Head Island encompasses a great variety of design styles. Though all are measured in yards, some are obviously more difficult than others. And, when you get down to measuring-stick basics, there are definitely some that stand far "taller" than others. The following list is a breakdown of the longest and the shortest for each standard par, including the highest and lowest ratings.

FROM THE PROFESSIONAL TEES

Longest Golf Course: Oyster Reef . . . . 7027 yards

Shortest Golf Course: Sea Pines Country Club . . . . 6346 yards
*Spanish Wells (Nine-Hole Layout) . . . . 6085 yards

Longest Par 5: No. 15 Long Cove . . . . 590 yards

Shortest Par 5: No. 10 Robber's Row . . . . 471 yards

Longest Par 4: No. 18 Harbourtown Golf Links . . . . 478 yards

Shortest Par 4: (Tie) No. 5 Long Cove . . . . 317 yards
No. 1 Robber's Row . . . . 317 yards

Longest Par 3: No. 17 George Fazio . . . . 230 yards

Shortest Par 3: No. 13 Long Cove . . . . 137 yards

Highest Course Rating: Long Cove 74.3

Lowest Course Rating: Sea Pines Country Club 70.7

Although these numbers show the longest and shortest holes, the holes themselves are not representative of the courses at which they are located. Long Cove, for example, has both the shortest par 4 and the shortest par 3, but it is in no way a short golf course.

The Facts

FROM THE WOMEN'S TEES

Longest Golf Course: Country Club of Hilton Head . . . . 5613 yards

Shortest Golf Course: Arthur Hills . . . . 4999 yards

Longest Par 5: No. 18 Country Club of Hilton Head . . . . . 507 yards

Shortest Par 5: No. 3 Spanish Wells . . . . 335 yards

Longest Par 4: No. 13 Country Club of Hilton Head . . . . . 393 yards

Shortest Par 4: No. 18 Wexford . . . . 225 yards

Longest Par 3: No. 7 Spanish Wells . . . . 179 yards

Shortest Par 3: No. 14 Country Club of Hilton Head . . . . . . 70 yards

Highest Course Rating: Country Club of Hilton Head 72

Lowest Course Rating: Arthur Hills 68.2

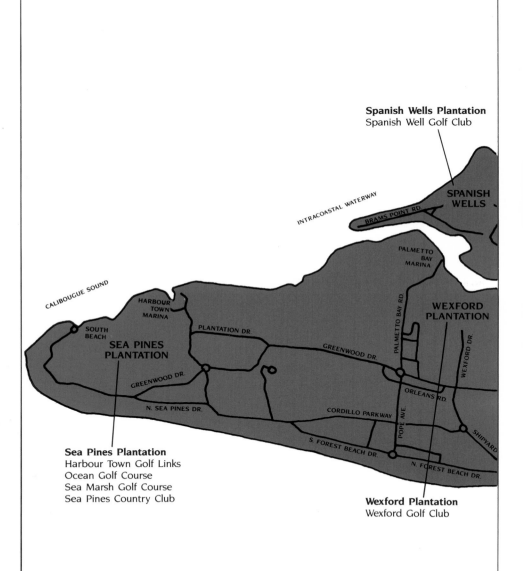

Spanish Wells Plantation
Spanish Well Golf Club

SPANISH WELLS

INTRACOASTAL WATERWAY

BRAMS POINT RD.

PALMETTO BAY MARINA

CALIBOUGUE SOUND

HARBOUR TOWN MARINA

WEXFORD PLANTATION

SOUTH BEACH

PLANTATION DR.

GREENWOOD DR.

PALMETTO BAY RD.

WEXFORD DR.

SEA PINES PLANTATION

GREENWOOD DR.

ORLEANS RD.

N. SEA PINES DR.

CORDILLO PARKWAY

POPE AVE.

SHIPYARD

S. FOREST BEACH DR.

N. FOREST BEACH DR.

Sea Pines Plantation
Harbour Town Golf Links
Ocean Golf Course
Sea Marsh Golf Course
Sea Pines Country Club

Wexford Plantation
Wexford Golf Club

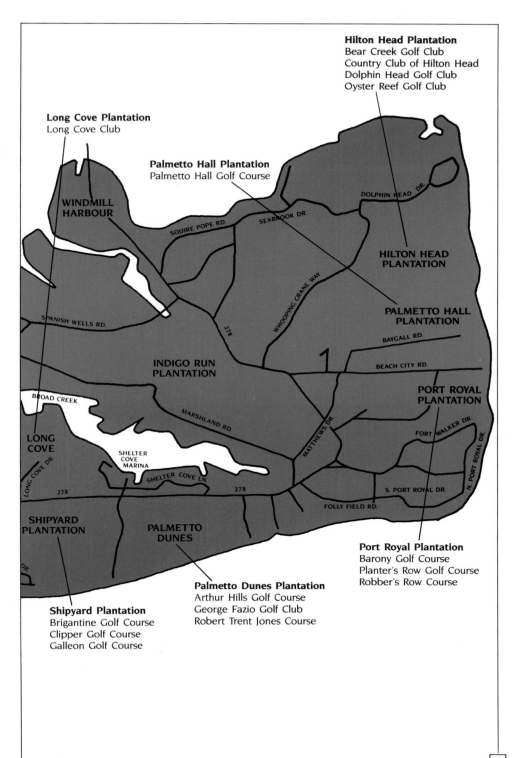

Hilton Head Plantation
Bear Creek Golf Club
Country Club of Hilton Head
Dolphin Head Golf Club
Oyster Reef Golf Club

Long Cove Plantation
Long Cove Club

Palmetto Hall Plantation
Palmetto Hall Golf Course

WINDMILL
HARBOUR

DOLPHIN HEAD DR.

SQUIRE POPE RD.   SEABROOK DR.

HILTON HEAD
PLANTATION

SPANISH WELLS RD.

WHOOPING CRANE WAY

278

PALMETTO HALL
PLANTATION

BAYGALL RD.

INDIGO RUN
PLANTATION

BEACH CITY RD.

BROAD CREEK

PORT ROYAL
PLANTATION

MARSHLAND RD.

FORT WALKER DR.

N. PORT ROYAL DR.

LONG
COVE

SHELTER
COVE
MARINA

LONG COVE DR.

MATTHEWS DR.

278   SHELTER COVE LN.   278

S. PORT ROYAL DR.

FOLLY FIELD RD.

SHIPYARD
PLANTATION

PALMETTO
DUNES

Port Royal Plantation
Barony Golf Course
Planter's Row Golf Course
Robber's Row Course

Palmetto Dunes Plantation
Arthur Hills Golf Course
George Fazio Golf Club
Robert Trent Jones Course

Shipyard Plantation
Brigantine Golf Course
Clipper Golf Course
Galleon Golf Course

Legends Guide to the Golf Courses of Hilton Head Island

Description: In this comprehensive guide to Hilton Head Island's golf courses every hole of every course is diagramed, pictured and described in full detail to give you the best explanation of all the magnificent golf holes.

How to use: The guide is a wonderful tool for planning the long awaited vacation to Hilton Head. Pick the courses, set up the tee times and plan your strategy on the layouts by studying the courses.

How to Order: Simply fill out the order form below. By ordering directly from the publisher, you will save $5.00.

_____
NAME

_____
STREET

_____
CITY   STATE   ZIP

 # Books Ordered   _____

x $35.00 per copy   _____

5% S.C. sales tax   _____

TOTAL   _____

Make checks payable to Legends Publications, Inc. Mail order form, along with check to:

Legends Publications, Inc.
Sales Dept.
39 New Orleans Road
Hilton Head Island, SC 29928

or call 803-842-2225 with credit card